The WE Movement was founded to give people the tools to make the world a better place. On our 25th anniversary, we offer this collection of stories from the field, where sustainable development programming in rural parts of India, Kenya and Ecuador is empowering families to shape their destinies. Without their courage and trust and the passion of a global network of supporters, we wouldn't have these stories to tell. This book is a testament to the value of every small action and the power of community to change the world.

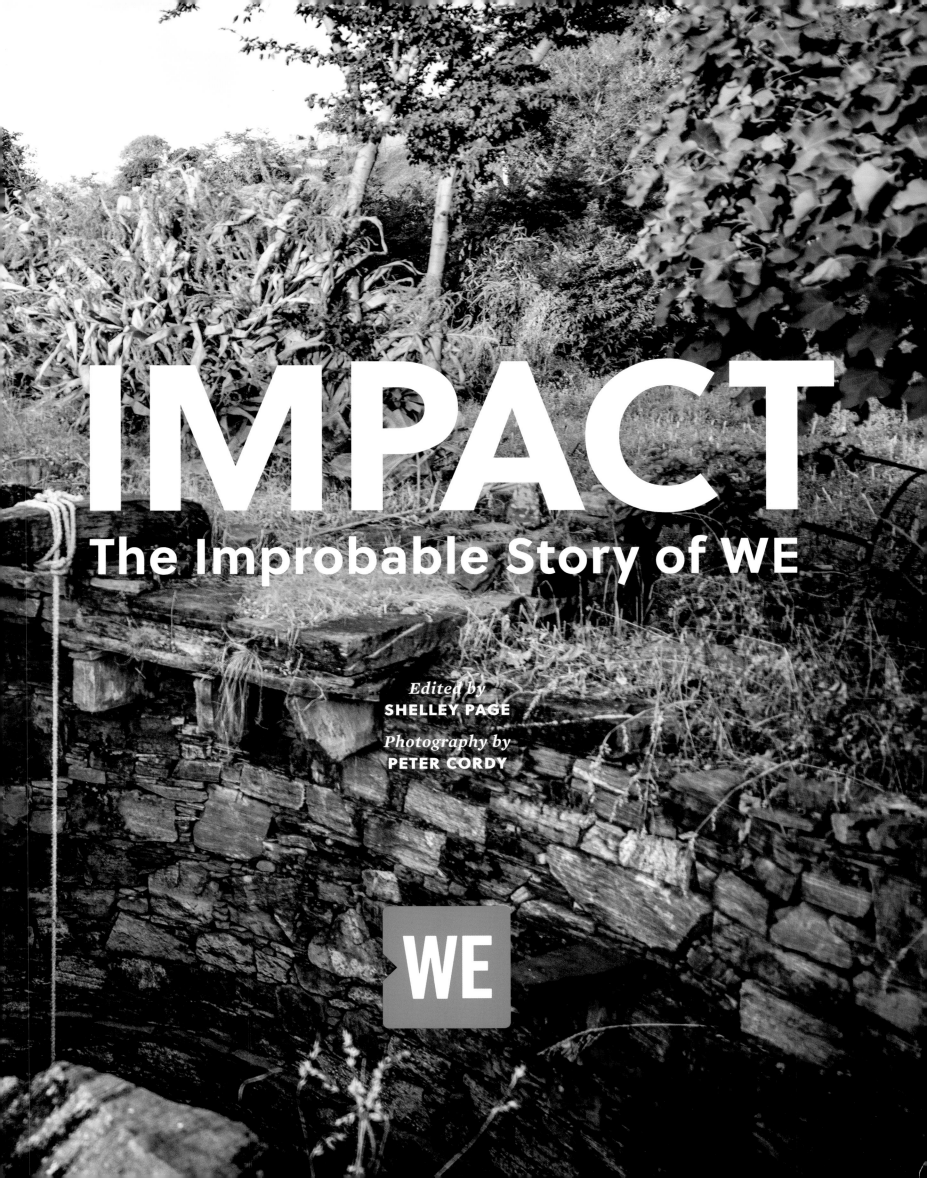

IMPACT
The Improbable Story of WE

Edited by
SHELLEY PAGE

Photography by
PETER CORDY

WE

A special thank you to Peter Cordy for his vision, stunning photography and financial support in bringing this book to life.

ISBN: 978-1-9991540-1-1
Cataloguing in publication information available upon request

WE CHARITY

339 Queen Street East
Toronto ON M5A 1S9
Canada

Learn more at WE.org

Distributed by WE Charity

Printed and bound in Canada by Friesens
Design by Counterpunch Inc. / Linda Gustafson

WE Charity is committed to reducing the consumption of old-growth forest in the books it publishes. This book is one step toward that goal.

IMPACT PHOTO CREDITS

All photography is by Peter Cordy, with the exception of:

Vito Amati: 10

Courtesy of Craig Burkinshaw: 307

Sara Cornthwaite: 15 (top left, and three on bottom right), 52, 53, 99 (top right and middle left), 206 (top right), 278 (top and bottom right), 282 (top right), 284 (top)

Karloso Fiallos: 229 (bottom left), 292 (top left), 293 (top right and bottom right)

Zeddy Kosgei: 127 (bottom row)

Victor Li: 294 (middle left and bottom left)

Reuben Muriuki: 126

Wanda O'Brien: 121 (bottom), 123 (top left), 207 (top left)

Courtesy of Kim Plewes: 304

Kim Plewes: 13 (top right), 15 (bottom left), 98 (top left), 99 (bottom right), 125, 127 (top), 166–167, 168, 169 (top right), 172 (bottom row), 184 (bottom), 205 (top), 206 (top left and bottom left), 294 (top)), 299 (all except top right), 302

Scott Ramsay: 14 (bottom left), 99 (top right), 207 (bottom right), 296 (middle left, bottom left), 299 (top right), 305

Courtesy of Phoebe Rotman: 301

WE Archives: xii, 2, 3, 4, 6, 8, 9, 11, 12 (all), 12 (all except top right), 14 (top row and bottom right), 98 (top right and bottom), 99 (middle right and bottom left), 206 (middle and bottom right), 207 (top right, middle and bottom left), 212, 292 (top right and bottom), 293 (top left, middle row, and bottom left), 294 (middle right, bottom middle and bottom right), 295 (all), 296 (top left, and all on right), 297 (all), 298 (all), 300, 303, 306, 309

This book was made possible through the extraordinary generosity of dear friends inspired by the impact of WE.

Contents

INDIA   18

KENYA 100

ECUADOR   208

Impact: The improbable story of WE

Behind every story in this book is a life transformed by WE Charity's sustainable impact, development delivered not through handouts but through partnership. This book is a tribute to the strength and wisdom of the communities we work with, the relentless passion of supporters around the globe, and our improbable journey together over 25 years.

BY CRAIG KIELBURGER AND MARC KIELBURGER, CO-FOUNDERS OF WE

Everyone told us it was impossible. We started as kids with fairly unrealistic goals—to empower ordinary people, especially young people, to tackle some of the world's most challenging problems. At first, we didn't want to start a charity. We cold-called existing charities asking how we could make a difference, and were told over and over that we were too young to help ... but did we know where our parents kept their credit cards? It's now been 25 years since we gathered classmates in our childhood living room and decided that twelve 12-year-olds could change the world. Looking back, our story does seem improbable.

When Craig first read a newspaper article about the murder of escaped child slave Iqbal Masih and began an after-school club to fight child labor, we couldn't predict that our work would spread around the world. Thanks to millions of people who joined in this effort, what started as a group of preteens has since grown into WE, a movement that makes doing good doable and proves anyone can change the world. The stories in this book are the result of the hope and hard work of countless partners, at home and in developing communities around the world. We are deeply humbled to share these stories with you.

You will read about the courageous women who form small business and financial literacy groups in tiny villages in Kenya, in places where women aren't traditional breadwinners. They break with custom, sometimes defying their husbands to earn extra income to send their children to school. We think of Jane Marindany, Rose Mutai and Judy Cheborkei, and the sacrifices they've endured to ensure their children are not laborers but rather educated community leaders.

We think of Milcah Chepkirui, a high school graduate of WE's Kisaruni Group of Schools in rural Kenya. As the 2019 valedictorian for the all-girls campus, she addressed hundreds of spectators gathered to celebrate girls who had overcome insurmountable odds to graduate that day. Many were the first generation of daughters in their families to attend high school, even to finish primary school. And until WE College opened in 2017, postsecondary education was a distant dream for most girls in rural Kenya.

We think of Miguel and Maria Bargas on the shores of the Napo River in Ecuador's Amazon rainforest. A lack of clean water was the likely cause of death for their 13-year-old daughter. The couple channeled their pain into activism, but limited resources thwarted their attempts to bring clean water to their community. Finally, in partnership with WE Charity, they created a water project to honor their daughter's memory.

We think of Kesi Bhil in Kamoda, Rajasthan, who once struggled to provide food and shelter for her family. When she joined a women's group with WE, she received financial literacy training and some very important assets—"super goats"—to launch a home business. But there was a catch. To join the group, members had to pledge to send their children to school. Though initially reluctant to enroll her children—who needed to work to support the household—Kesi has learned to save on a monthly basis, added protein-rich goat milk to her family's diet, and finally built them a house of their own.

Behind every story in this book is a life transformed by sustainable impact, development work done in partnership with community members. This book is a tribute to their strength and commitment, and to our journey together.

It started in April of 1995.

Kids Helping Kids

Iqbal Masih stared out at Craig from the front page of our hometown newspaper. Then 12 years old, Craig had picked up the paper to find the comics section, starting his day as usual with a bowl of cereal and *Calvin and Hobbes*. But on this day, April 19, he couldn't take his eyes off the headline: "Battled child labor, boy, 12, murdered."

Craig Kielburger (back row, center), started WE Charity in 1995 when he was 12 years old, along with his older brother, Marc Kielburger (not pictured), and a group of classmates. One of the charity's first acts was to petition for the release of child rights activist Kailash Satyarthi, then imprisoned in India. Craig and his friends collected 3,000 signatures and mailed the petition to India in a shoebox.

Children march to protest child labor in India during the time of Craig's trip to Southeast Asia. At age 13, Craig traveled to India and Pakistan, among other countries, to research the issue of child labor.

Marc (right) with his father, Fred. The first WE Charity headquarters occupied the Kielburger family living room.

Iqbal lived in Pakistan. When he was four years old, his parents sold him into slavery for less than US$12. For six years he was shackled to a carpet-weaving loom as he worked, tying tiny knots in intricate designs. He managed to break free, at the age of 10, and traveled the world speaking out against child labor. Two years after his escape, he was shot dead while he and two friends were riding their bikes in their village of Muridke, outside Lahore. It was suspected that Iqbal was killed by his former captors, who sought to silence him.

The story transported Iqbal's shockingly unjust world to our breakfast table and upended our middle-class lives. It was the first we had heard about child labor.

Craig took Iqbal's story to his Grade 7 class and asked who would help, and 11 hands shot up. We originally called ourselves the "group of twelve 12-year-olds." The name lasted approximately one week, until one of us had a 13th birthday. We like to joke that somehow we didn't see that coming. We became Free The Children, and finally WE, which includes WE Charity and the social enterprise ME to WE.

Marc is five years older and at the time of our founding had just finished high school. He quickly became a mentor for the pint-sized group of activists. Years later, Marc would juggle the charity's work while pursuing his education at Harvard, followed by a Rhodes Scholarship to study law at Oxford University, while Craig became the youngest-ever graduate of the Kellogg-Schulich executive MBA. We both eschewed traditional career paths to grow the impact of our children's charity, something we could never have done without the unfailing support of our family.

We owe our parents, Fred and Theresa, a huge debt of gratitude. They are the greatest unsung heroes of WE Charity, an organization that wouldn't exist today without their incredible dedication.

Before we were born, Mom took a few years off from teaching to work as an outreach worker, helping homeless youth escape drugs, alcoholism and prostitution. Dad slept on Jean Vanier's office couch while volunteering one summer at the original L'Arche, a home for adults with developmental disabilities in Trosly-Breuil, France. Our parents didn't talk much about their own activism, so we learned these stories only as we grew older and asked questions. It wasn't their style to tell us how to do things, but they still got a lot of grief from others who were critical of their "indulgence" of two teenagers with dreams of improving the world. Many years later, it's become the norm for young people to get involved in complex social issues, but that wasn't the case back then. Though we've always been grateful, we didn't fully appreciate their sacrifice until we had our own kids. Our parents turned their lives upside down for us. More than that, they gave us their trust and respect, enough to explore the world and our passions. And they taught us to fight for what we believe in, no matter how hard it seems. Over the years, we've been honored to meet many world leaders and Nobel laureates, but our parents are our greatest heroes.

In the early days, as our tiny charity found its footing, Mom and Dad chauffeured us everywhere, taught us basic accounting and offered in-kind donations of frozen lasagna. In the years ahead, they would give up one room of their house after another for our office space, and then finally moved out entirely to live in the home of our late grandfather while we converted the whole family house into the charity's headquarters. In the years that followed, Mom and Dad would take early retirement from their teaching positions to dedicate themselves full-time to the charity, helping with any and every role imaginable. Our heartfelt gratitude goes to our mother, Theresa, who is one of the most capable and humble leaders we've ever met, with an uncanny ability to nurture talent and help young people succeed. Many of today's senior leaders within the organization grew up with her mentorship and guidance. When our parents finally sold

During Craig's research trip to Asia, he secured a meeting with Canada's then prime minister Jean Chrétien (center) to discuss Canada's commitment to ending child labor and global poverty.

Craig in the Filipino capital of Manila

our family home, they used the funds to purchase a proper space for the organization's office, which they provided rent-free for over a decade, until external donations funded WE Charity's purchase of the WE Global Learning Centre. Mom and Dad have provided more in-kind support, labor and dedication than is possible to measure. We could write volumes expressing our gratitude. They taught us everything we know about giving back.

Unaccompanied Minor

When our charity was less than a year old, Craig planned a research trip to Southeast Asia, a seven-week odyssey with proposed stops in Thailand, India, Nepal and Pakistan, to see the issue of child labor first-hand and find the best project to finance. Our parents had other ideas about their youngest son skipping almost two months of school to travel overseas, mostly to destinations with travel advisories attached.

"You're only 12," our mom told Craig with a sigh. "You've never even been on the subway alone. You're not going to Asia."

After months of Craig pestering, shoveling snowy driveways to save money, scouting a suitable chaperone, contacting local agencies, and assembling a medical kit that rivalled those issued by the military, Mom and Dad allowed him to go to Asia. They always believed in the mission of the organization, even as it was evolving, even when it seemed impossible.

Craig's trip would have profound consequences for the rest of our lives. He joined activists on an emotional journey to return freed child slaves to their homes, met Iqbal Masih's mother in Pakistan to tell her that her son's life and death had inspired a movement, and spent time with Mother Teresa in Calcutta, who told him, "You can do no great things, only small things with great love."

Halfway through the trip, Craig learned that Canada's then prime minister Jean Chrétien was traveling in Asia on a trade delegation. At 13, Craig held a press conference in the lobby of Chrétien's hotel, inviting two freed child slaves. It caused quite the commotion in the media, and afterwards Craig was able to secure a meeting with the Prime Minister to discuss increasing Canada's commitment to ending global poverty. In the years that followed, because of our advocacy, the Canadian and Italian governments would pass legislation to enable the domestic prosecution of their nationals who were found guilty of exploiting children overseas, while the Brazilian government increased their funding commitments to education programs for former child laborers.

That early trip also inspired our first big commitment as a charity. By this point, we had raised over C$150,000, and decided our funds would go to establish Bal Ashram, a counseling center for freed child slaves in India. This would be our first and last rescue center. The rescue workers kicked down factory doors and led bewildered children into the sunshine, then on to rehabilitation and their parents. But when the same children were sold back into slavery because of their families' crippling poverty, we quickly realized we couldn't facilitate physical freedom without presenting an alternative to labor. But what could we offer as a recourse, as a skill that would endure—an education? Could we free children by empowering families to lift themselves out of poverty? These questions would eventually lead to our five-pillar development model and would dramatically improve the lives of people in communities where we'd come to work. Our very idea of freedom had changed.

TOP: *Marc with two friends in Bangkok, Thailand, where he volunteered in an AIDS hospice. Then a teenager, Marc spent months caring for patients as they took their last breaths. The trip helped inspire his commitment to social justice.*
BOTTOM (BOTH PHOTOS): *During his research trip to Southeast Asia, Craig discussed the issue of child slavery with many of the children he met. Some of those children were engaged in forms of labor, including brick breaking and carpet weaving.*

A Mogul Mentor

The Oprah Winfrey Show asked Craig, when he was 16, to appear on an episode featuring young people making a positive difference in the world. Oprah, being Oprah, had prepared a surprise for each guest. A young New Jersey boy whose school had held a fundraiser came out to present Craig with a giant novelty check for US$3,378 to help build a school in Nicaragua.

Instead of wrapping up the segment, Oprah paused, then said something that would alter the course of our lives. "You know what?" she announced. "I want to build a hundred schools with you."

The show cut to a commercial break. Craig was in shock, mouth agape, and he wasn't alone. Showrunners, producers and lawyers swarmed around Oprah, advising her to reshoot the segment without the final unplanned surprise. She hadn't vetted us, and yet she'd made a very public promise. But Oprah had made up her mind. This would be her first major overseas investment.

Oprah's team asked Craig to return with "adult supervision" to discuss the terms of this large donation. For the second meeting, Marc came along, directly from his college class. A second-year university student, he brought along his then girlfriend (and future wife, lawyer and ME to WE Artisans founder), Roxanne Joyal. This wasn't the adult leadership that the largest media mogul in the world had in mind. Oprah's team hammered us with questions: "Do your schools have paraseismic engineers? Do you do currency hedges to make sure fluctuations don't affect the final price of your projects? Do you have third-party governance and evaluation systems in place?"

At the time, WE Charity had built a few dozen schools. The charity was still operating out of our parents' house. We had a single phone line. But we also possessed a lot of stubbornness and idealism. Oprah and her team approached our partnership like venture capitalists, pushing us to grow and deliver scalable social change using a model similar to a successful tech company, not a cash-poor charity. Oprah would feature our work in five more shows over the next decade, and Oprah's Angel Network invested heavily in our physical and administrative infrastructure. She assisted us with sourcing the best engineers to build schools that would withstand earthquakes in South America and years of monsoon seasons in Asia. Beyond her promise to construct schools, she built up our resources behind the scenes, funding the best logistics experts, auditing firms, measurement agencies, and local consultants who provided on-the-ground support in each country. Looking back, Oprah helped us set foundations to not only change lives but create sustainable impact that would continue long after WE transitioned out of our partner communities. We couldn't have asked for a better mentor or guardian angel. Twenty-odd years later, Oprah's schools are still standing in every one of the countries where we work.

WE Charity's Oleleshwa Farm in Kenya's Maasai Mara sits on more than 30 acres of land and features 14 greenhouses. Part of the charity's food pillar, the farm provides lunches for local schools and offers agricultural training for smallholder farmers to help improve their own plots, crop yields and nutrition intake.

Each new school was cause for tremendous celebration. Entire communities filled our small campuses to watch ribbon cuttings and see the spaces where their children would learn, in most cases the first generation in their families to get an education. With Oprah-funded measurement systems in place, we diligently tracked the impact of every project. We were surprised when, months after a school opened, attendance started to dwindle. Girls were dropping out in virtually every country in which we worked. We quickly realized that in many developing communities, girls are responsible for fetching water, often from miles away, a task that can consume an entire school day. Building a school wasn't enough. Elders and leaders in our partner communities identified other challenges. So much of our early work was cemented around these conversations and coming to understand that everything is interconnected.

With advice from our community partners, WE Charity built rainwater catchment systems. We dug boreholes hundreds of feet into the earth to coax out groundwater, then installed hand pumps next to our schools, central locations where families could easily collect water, especially girls on their way home from class. Over the years, even our water projects grew with us, as we added solar-powered generators for larger pumps and state-of-the-art filtration systems. Bouts of malaria and tuberculosis were the genesis of our health pillar, which now includes preventative health education, mobile and permanent clinics, and even a full hospital with surgery facilities and a state-of-the-art maternity wing.

Malnutrition in some of our overseas partner communities was extreme. We established large-scale agricultural production areas, allowing us to implement school lunch programs. Following the old adage about teaching a (wo)man to fish, we planted vegetable gardens on our campuses, making agricultural training part of the curriculum. Children now learn farming techniques at school from local specialists, taking the findings home to their parents' fields. In the majority of these regions, smallholding farms with a few cash crops are the most common source of income.

When people are healthy and well fed, and women are free from the burden of carrying river water for miles, they have more time to work and provide for their families. The final pillar of our development model was an alternative income program in the form of business training and community-led microloan groups. Tens of thousands of small businesses were seeded, growing local economies and giving families the financial stability needed to send their kids to school and break the cycle of poverty.

It took us years to hone this model, and the final step was to put ourselves out of business. Five to eight years after the start of our partnerships, we want communities to take ownership of their progress. Reliance on us is not a solution; WE Charity is designed to create sustainable impact that makes our continued oversight obsolete. Sustainable impact means empowering our partner communities to lift themselves out of poverty, and to function independently of us. Our definition of success is for the community to implement all five pillars, as well as training sessions to continue forward momentum. Once the flywheel to end poverty is built, local leaders continue to increase its speed through their own leadership and compounding economic growth.

But in order to make a commitment for five-plus years where we work, we needed a guaranteed source of steady funding. We needed

Roxanne Joyal (center), CEO of ME to WE, with her youngest daughter, Violette, and two women from the ME to WE Artisans program, which connects women entrepreneurs in rural regions where employment is scarce with a wider market to sell their traditional beadwork.

to guard against economic downturns and changing donor cycles. A financial safety net would ensure long-term project funding and give us room to experiment with our development model, to take risks on innovative approaches that would yield greater impact.

ME to WE Social Enterprise started as a means to empower Maasai communities in Kenya. We sought to get Maasai goods to a wider market, to support the Kenyan artisans who hand-beaded beautiful jewelry in their traditional designs but had few customers. As of 2020, 1,600 women entrepreneurs in Kenya, beading a variety of products for ME to WE's Artisans, earned an average of four times more than their previous wages.

The majority of ME to WE's net profits, including from the sales of ME to WE Artisans products and ME to WE licensed products, are donated back to WE Charity, with the balance reinvested to grow the social enterprise and its mission. As of 2020, more than C$20 million had been donated to WE Charity by ME to WE since it launched in 2007. This revenue supports hard-to-fund projects, like administrative tasks that donors don't typically find sexy or appealing but are still necessary to keep a charity running. Money from ME to WE sales supports projects in the artisans' home villages (as well as other projects around the world), which means that women entrepreneurs earn fair wages while also funding transformational development right where they live. Many of the artisan women are mothers whose

skills fund the construction of their children's schools, for instance.

This social enterprise model has allowed WE to redefine certain aspects of the traditional charitable model. WE Charity has never had to spend precious dollars on traditional fundraising mechanisms such as street canvassers, phone-bank systems or Sunday morning commercials. Instead, consumers purchase ME to WE products from thousands of partner retail locations and learn about the social mission in-store. Instead of a charity paying to promote its brand, customers pay to place our products in their kitchen cupboards, or under the Christmas tree, or to wear our brand and share the message with their friends. As a result of this unique way to grow our brand, our charity's administration rate, at 10 percent, is well below the industry average. We can proudly tell our donors and partner communities that 90 cents of every dollar goes directly to support projects.

ME to WE also allows us to invest in unique programs to further the social mission. For example, ME to WE Trips have given over 40,000 of our stakeholders the chance to visit those very same projects, providing a level of transparency that connects them directly to the communities and lives changed through their generous support. Similarly, our "Track Your Impact" technology adds a unique code to each ME to WE Artisans product or ME to WE licensed product that consumers can enter online to see the social impact created through their purchase, and where the proceeds from sales

Veronica Yasaca is a member of the inaugural girls' club in San Miguel, Ecuador. The leadership program helps teenage girls finance their high school studies to stay in school while building confidence and self-esteem.

Nashilu Dapash earns a sustainable income working with ME to WE Artisans, crafting traditional Maasai jewelry from intricate glass beads. The program now employs more than 1,600 women.

were delivered—geotagged and pinpointed on a map. We believe in transparency, that anyone should be able to travel, physically or virtually, to see the impact they've created along with us.

ME to WE has since expanded into artisans programs in Ecuador, as well as launching a consumables line with chocolate and coffee. In the years after the start of these partnerships, thousands of well-paying jobs in remote developing communities have been created in agriculture (ME to WE's Fair Trade–certified chocolate), hospitality and tourism (with ME to WE Trips to where WE Charity works, such as Kenya, India and Ecuador), and, of course, the artisan entrepreneurs.

Thanks to this economic empowerment, when our teams transition out, communities continue to move forward on all key indicators: lower infant mortality rates, higher graduation rates and more gender parity in work outside the home. That's not charity; it's sustainable impact.

This book is a celebration of 25 years of sustainable impact, with so much of it delivered in unconventional ways—not through temporary handouts but through partnerships. If not for the women in Kenya who took a risk on us and joined our first artisans programs, WE Charity wouldn't have the freedom to experiment, to tap into the for-profit sector and leverage the resources and infrastructure of huge companies now committed to giving back.

WE Charity's impact by the numbers

200,000 children empowered by 1,500 schools built

30,000 women who have achieved financial independence through opportunity programs

15M meals produced by the farmers we work with

1M people have gained access to clean water

C$36M worth of medical supplies provided to communities where WE Charity partners

A Reckoning

To empower people to lift themselves out of poverty and create sustainable impact, you have to untangle every thread. Anything else is a bandage solution. Honed over 25 years, our development model now has five pillars that are mutually reinforcing: education, clean water, health, opportunity and food security.

Once that model is fully implemented and flourishing, local leaders can and should take over, with a clear idea of what progress means to them. When that happens, we're more than happy to admit that we're no longer needed. WE Charity has so far transitioned out of 21 communities around the world. One of those communities is Salabwek, in Kenya's Maasai Mara.

Before WE Charity's partnership with Salabwek, the village had no source of clean water. The literacy rate was 10 percent, and school buildings were primarily mud huts, hot and leaky and structurally unsound. The average family income was less than US$1 per day. Five years after WE Charity exited Salabwek, the community underwent an independent third-party study by Mission Measurement, a Chicago-based firm that tracks social impact. At the local primary school, there were 20 new buildings, with concrete foundations, proper ventilation and waterproofing. With school more accessible and more appealing, the number of girls graduating, now able to attend high school, had increased to 50 percent from 27 percent. A water catchment system and piping had been installed at the school; maintenance and training were ongoing, led by the local water committee. The number of households with access to clean water had increased by 80 percent. Salabwek's village savings-and-loan program was yielding a 15 percent annual return, handsome profit margins for any investor, anywhere in the world. School and community farm projects had led to a 26 percent increase in the number of children with access to nutritious food. And, most incredibly, a new clinic and preventative health education program had boosted access to health care by 98 percent. All key indicators are moving in the right direction.

It's worth repeating that the study was conducted five years *after* WE Charity stopped working in the community, which means

Craig lays bricks for a WE Charity construction project with Malala Yousafzai in Kenya's Maasai Mara. Malala, a Pakistani activist, was shot by the Taliban at age 14 for her vocal support of girls' education. At age 17, she was awarded the Nobel Peace Prize. Malala is one of many visitors to travel with WE to volunteer support for WE Charity's projects around the world.

Students in Ecuador's mountain province of Chimborazo tend to their school garden. Here in the Andean mountains, growing conditions are harsh, and many people are smallholder farmers. WE Charity offers agricultural training at schools, where children learn techniques to help in their parents' plots. When household yields and incomes improve, children have more prospects after graduation.

Salabwek is self-sustaining. Local leaders continue to maintain projects, conduct training and implement programming. We can't overstate the importance of this achievement—a success for Salabwek, not for us. And though the accomplishment comes with joyful pride, these are objective, numerical findings that prove the transformative nature of WE Charity's five-pillar development model. With enough grit, continuous learning and shared determination, it is possible to empower people to lift themselves out of poverty.

And it is possible for those empowered to pay it forward. People in our partner communities often share their learnings with others, their families and friends and even neighbors in surrounding villages. In Ecuador's mountainous province of Chimborazo, students in Shuid are teaching their parents about targeted irrigation and crop variety. WE Charity's agricultural trainers offer lessons to the students at Shuid Primary School, and the kids take those lessons back home to their parents and friends. Capacity building for farming practices is also common in India, where crop yields have more than

doubled in regions where our team works. Kitchen gardens at home use the techniques taught to children at school, who also give their parents, aunts, uncles and friends in neighboring schools lessons on healthy habits, improving nutrition and health among families, neighborhoods and whole regions. These shared learnings among communities will feed families for generations.

Girls attending high school at the Kisaruni Group of Schools in Kenya are also studying agriculture, bringing lessons back home and sharing skills to improve their families' crop yields. In order to graduate, they must also complete a capstone service project, and many choose to promote awareness about girls' rights and early childhood marriage, even traveling to other schools, clearing the path for girls to go to school in as many communities as they can reach. In regions that are typically recipients of aid, students are empowered to lead their own change. Having young people take up our work and bring that change to others is truly collaborative and sustainable impact.

Craig and Marc onstage at WE Day, a global youth empowerment event held in a series of cities around the world. Students can't buy tickets but instead must earn their way to the shows, which feature prominent world leaders as well as the latest pop stars, all celebrating the social impact created through the WE Schools program.

Home Team

When the United Nations outlined its Sustainable Development Goals (SDGs) in 2015, there was an urgent call for partnership in the fight to end global poverty, a call for international cooperation of governments, the private sector and individual citizens to accelerate progress. While all of the goals require cooperation, SDG 17 is dedicated to strengthening partnerships for sustainable development. WE strives to help meet that goal in many ways, most especially by engaging a new generation. This book is focused on our international projects, but we cannot end global poverty by focusing exclusively on the Global South. We must also look at policies, practices and norms in the Global North, and part of that means raising a generation of active and compassionate global change-makers.

The next generation of idealistic youth is emerging from our WE Schools program, a service-learning model in the United States, Canada, the United Kingdom and, increasingly, other countries, that links volunteering with core classroom curriculum to support not just our campaigns but any cause. The chance for kids all over the world to give back through a program that teaches the value of responsible citizenship is, for us, one of the most incredible parts of our programming. Young people are learning about sustainable development, local activism and capacity building, wherever they live. Girls at Kisaruni are raising awareness of women's rights. Meanwhile, kids in North America are engaged in service learning. Our WE Schools program reaches more than four million students

every year with practical lessons that also give back, including a partnership with the College Board that bakes service learning into Advanced Placement (AP) courses for credit. Our AP with WE Service program is the first on-transcript recognition of volunteer service in America. Students are testing water purity levels in science classes and starting letter-writing campaigns to push politicians to better protect natural resources. They're launching school-wide food drives to support the homeless, as well as initiatives to save their local library branch from funding cuts. And they're sharing goals and successes with their peers across oceans.

Part of ending global poverty is raising awareness among a generation that's poised to make the most impact. Empowering young people to connect and inspire each other was the genesis behind WE Day, a stadium-sized event held in dozens of cities around the world. Since the early days, WE Day has filled some historic venues—from the Forum in California to Barclays Center in New York to Wembley Arena in London—welcoming more than one million youth attendees and reaching millions more with prime-time TV broadcasts on ABC and MTV. These events bring together world leaders, pop culture icons and young activists to celebrate young people leading the change. You can't buy a ticket to WE Day; students earn entry through volunteer service—not just for WE, but for any cause they care about. Since its launch, WE Schools participants engaged in our service-learning program have logged more than 46 million volunteer hours and raised C$119 million for local and global causes. In fact, more than 80 percent of youth fundraising dollars go to non-profits and causes that aren't affiliated with WE, such as the Terry Fox Foundation, Ronald McDonald House and the SPCA.

Craig and Marc visiting a WE Charity school in India.

Milestones

WE Charity has worked in over 45 countries around the world, with full five-pillar WE Village models implemented over the years in Sierra Leone, Ethiopia, Kenya, Tanzania, India, Sri Lanka, China, Nicaragua, Haiti, the Dominican Republic and Ecuador. But we chose to focus this book on one country for each of the continents of Asia, Africa and Latin America—India, Kenya and Ecuador—for important reasons. Our learnings while working in these countries shaped our very approach to development.

In India, where we first kicked down factory doors to rescue child slaves only to find them sold back into labor, we learned the difference between a stopgap measure and a sustainable solution. Our partner communities in India helped expand our methods and test multi-pronged tactics, leading to our five-pillar model.

In Kenya, we discovered the importance of social enterprise as a tool to preserve and celebrate culture. Maasai customs in Kenya helped shape our core operations on a grand scale, and the country became our second home as we scaled our model. Maasai women and their traditional beadwork inspired our social enterprise, and we spent so much time with these communities that they became extended family. Each of us was honored to have a traditional Maasai wedding, and we still visit often, now with our own children.

In Ecuador, we learned about the concept of *minga* from the indigenous Kichwa people. We realized that this custom, roughly translated as "people coming together in the common good"—to harvest a field or raise a roof—needed to be brought back home with us, to help us forge deeper connections as a movement. The philosophy inspired our creation of WE Days and so much of our core mission, vision and values.

It is customary to keep thank-yous in the acknowledgments section, but we couldn't help but write a short note of gratitude here as well. To our dedicated staff, our board members and our generous supporters—we thank you. Humbly we ask our stakeholders to continue their support for communities in India, Kenya, Ecuador and the other countries where we work. As you'll see from the stories in the following pages, these partnerships are truly life changing. Our biggest hope for the future is more lives changed through sustainable impact.

WE Charity launched in 1995 with limited assets—12 kids, a fax machine and a Commodore 64 computer. When the WE Global Learning Center, our global headquarters, opened its doors in Toronto in 2017, visitors found four floors in a brick-and-beam heritage building, equipped with Skype pods where visiting students can speak with sister schools overseas and educators enjoy a much-deserved moment of calm in the lobby café, which brews up Fair Trade coffee from ME to WE, with beans grown by farmers in WE Charity's partner communities. In the middle of the city, it's a truly global hub. Our charity has come a long way from our parents' kitchen table.

We are incredibly proud to share the inspiring photos of our community partners and the transformative stories of sustainable impact held between the covers of this book. Thank you to all who have made this work possible.

After WE Schools and WE Day, family and corporate resources were developed as we tailored offerings for those groups. Now people come to WE to discover their own causes and take on more meaningful actions through educational resources, and also through volunteer travel.

Nothing cements partnerships and fosters connections for people in different countries quite like cultural immersion. ME to WE Trips has so far hosted over 40,000 travelers, youth and families learning about global development while creating jobs in ecotourism in our various partner communities. This is our biggest shared learning opportunity, where our international partners showcase their culture and travelers learn about sustainable development, its methods, challenges and successes. Their guides and teachers are community leaders and in-country experts who are always there to answer questions. We have received thousands of letters from students and families who say that our trips have changed their lives, altered their courses of study, and shifted their ideas about citizenship and community. But we have more proof than just their letters. A Mission Measurement study found that trip participants were more likely to volunteer and vote, even over the long term. When our WE Schools students and our travelers think globally, international partnerships improve on a larger scale.

Milestones in the evolution of WE

1995

April 16. Twelve-year-old Iqbal Masih—an escaped child laborer who told his story to the world—is murdered in his village in Pakistan. Three days later, 12-year-old Craig Kielburger reads about Iqbal in the *Toronto Star* and is moved to take action on the issue of child labor. He and 11 classmates start "Free The Children," operating from the Kielburger family home and under the mentorship of Craig's older brother, Marc.

1995

After a summer of holding neighborhood fundraisers, the group commits to building a charity and international movement of young people standing up for children's rights. Craig is the keynote speaker at the Ontario Federation of Labour, where attendees pledge CA$150,000 to build a rehabilitation center for rescued child laborers.

1995

December 9. Craig embarks on a seven-week research trip across South Asia to learn about the experiences of working children. Alongside his friend and chaperone, 25-year-old Alam Rahman, he meets hundreds of children working in dangerous conditions and vows to share their stories.

1996

April 21. The television news magazine *60 Minutes* features Free The Children. The next day, the organization's email system crashes because of the overwhelming response.

1998

Donations to Free The Children (later rebranded "WE Charity") fund its first schools in the mountainous region of Waslala, Nicaragua, and in West Bengal, India. In subsequent years, the organization breaks ground for schools in Kenya and Ecuador.

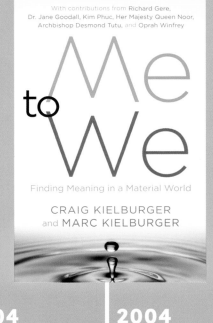

1998

November 7. Craig publishes his first best-selling book, *Free the Children*, sharing stories of the working children he met in South Asia.

1999

Craig makes his first appearance on *The Oprah Winfrey Show*, where Winfrey commits to helping the organization build more than 60 new schools around the world.

2000

Craig and Marc host their first youth volunteer trip to Kenya to help create meaningful connections between travelers and local residents and inspire new actions. Today, thousands of guests, including youth, school groups, families and corporate groups, travel with ME to WE Trips to visit WE Charity development projects in communities around the world.

2004

Building on previous development work, WE Charity launches a holistic and sustainable development model that evolves to include five pillars that address the root causes of child labor, providing education, clean water, health, income opportunity and food security programs that work together to help families lift themselves from poverty.

2004

Craig and Marc Kielburger publish their best-selling book *Me to We: Finding Meaning in a Material World*. They later establish ME to WE Social Enterprises to offer socially conscious products and experiences, including international volunteer trips, creating a sustainable revenue stream to support WE Charity.

Milestones in the evolution of WE

2004

ME to WE opens Bogani Cottages and Tented Camp near the Maasai Mara National Reserve, serving as a base for international volunteer groups visiting WE Charity projects in Kenya.

2007

Roxanne Joyal, who was integral to the evolution of WE Charity, founds ME to WE Artisans to help Maasai women gain access to a global market for their traditional beadwork. Today, ME to WE Artisans provides women in Kenya and Ecuador with a sustainable income, empowering them within their households and community and helping them send their children to school.

2008

WE Charity partners with the community of San Miguel, Ecuador, to build new classrooms for the existing primary school and plan for a high school. In 2015, the community celebrates the first group of high school graduates.

2011

WE Charity establishes Baraka Health Clinic to provide health care services for communities in rural Narok County, Kenya. In 2013, the clinic opens a maternity wing to support maternal and infant health. In 2017, the health clinic is officially recognized as Baraka Hospital with the opening of a surgical unit and inpatient wing that further serves the health care needs of the region.

2013

ME to WE opens Minga Lodge in the Amazon region of Ecuador and Araveli Cottages and Tented Camp in Rajasthan, India, welcoming international visitors and volunteers to contribute directly to WE Charity projects and connect with partner communities.

2014

The all-girls campus of the Kisaruni Group of Schools, established in 2010 in rural Kenya, celebrates its first graduating class. When Kenya's national exam results are released, Kisaruni ranks first out of 112 secondary schools in Narok County.

2015

WE Charity completes a three-year agriculture and food security pilot project with 80 farmers in rural Rajasthan, India. Results show that participants are 100% food secure at the end of the program. This pilot project leads to the organization's food security programming in India, so farmers can move from subsistence to cultivating cash crops and growing more nutritious food.

2016

WE Charity opens the Mondaña Health Clinic in the Amazon region of Ecuador, having partnered with the Ministry of Health to fully rebuild the structure to offer maternal health, outpatient and dental services. The clinic also becomes the base for mobile clinics, providing outreach programs to surrounding communities.

2017

WE College opens in Narok County, Kenya, with the School of Tourism and the School of Nursing, expanding the educational opportunities available to students in the Maasai Mara region. Many WE College scholarship recipients attended WE Charity–supported primary schools and studied at the Kisaruni Group of Schools.

2018

WE Charity opens the Agriculture Learning Center in Ecuador's Amazon region, enhancing local traditions with new techniques, tools and knowledge to improve farmers' yields and preserve rainforest biodiversity.

2019

WE College celebrates the first graduating class in tourism and hospitality. The occasion is marked by an official ribbon-cutting ceremony attended by H.E. Margaret Kenyatta, First Lady of the Republic of Kenya.

WE Charity's Five Pillars of sustainable development

WE Charity believes in a world where all children have access to education and where families are empowered with the means and the opportunities to achieve their goals. Guided by this mission, the organization partners with rural communities to help equip them with the knowledge and tools to improve their quality of life. Creating sustainable impact requires a holistic approach that considers the multiple challenges that give rise to poverty and presents lasting solutions. Anything less is merely a stopgap.

Honed over 25 years, WE Charity's development model has five pillars that are mutually reinforcing and respond to basic needs and rights: education, water, health, food and opportunity. This unique model evolved through extensive consultation and collaboration with rural community members, local governments and international development experts. It works by leveraging a community's existing strengths—skills and traditions cultivated over generations—and helping to build further capabilities. Community members are involved in the design and implementation of programs and help tailor projects to meet their specific realities. By investing time and resources in new initiatives, they assume ownership of the programs and learn the skills needed to keep them going for generations.

The ultimate goal of WE Charity's five-pillar model is to achieve sustainable impact, whereby communities are empowered to maintain and evolve projects—from schools and water systems to nutrition programs and small businesses— independent of outside support. In other words, WE Charity is in the business of putting itself out of business.

★ EDUCATION

Education is the best way to equip communities with the knowledge and tools to improve their quality of life.
Education programs include:
- Building schoolrooms, libraries, offices and teacher accommodations
- Rehabilitating existing school infrastructure
- Providing desks, chairs and supplies
- Training teachers
- Establishing extracurricular and leadership programs

◊ WATER

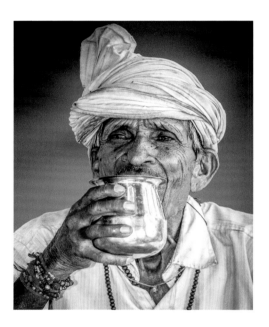

Access to clean water frees girls from the daily burden of collecting water for their families, allowing them to attend school and preventing waterborne illnesses.
Water programs include:
- Creating clean water systems, including drilling boreholes and rehabilitating wells
- Building handwashing stations and latrines
- Providing workshops in basic hygiene and waterborne disease prevention

HEALTH

Children can attend school only if they are healthy and if their families have access to health care and information.

Health programs include:

- Providing basic medical supplies
- Facilitating mobile health clinics and direct health care services
- Offering preventative health workshops

FOOD

Children can succeed in school only if they have the energy to focus. Undernourished children are at best inattentive and at worst ill.

Food programs include:

- Providing agriculture training and tools to smallholding farmers
- Creating irrigation systems
- Supplying seeds and guidance for families to plant protein-rich crops
- Establishing school gardens and nutrition programs

OPPORTUNITY

Children can attend school only if their parents have the financial means to invest in their education.

Opportunity programs include:

- Improving or creating income-generation avenues for parents, such as animal husbandry or handicrafts
- Establishing savings collectives and microenterprise groups
- Offering business and financial literacy training

INDIA

From long-haul flights to factories to five pillars

"Our improbable journey began in India, where we learned about the complexity of development and first shaped WE Charity's five pillars, which work in tandem to lift families out of poverty."

BY CRAIG KIELBURGER, CO-FOUNDER OF WE

Pinned to the wall of our first WE Charity office in our parents' converted garage was a huge map of the world. As kids, we mailed dozens of letters to human rights organizations in countries all over the map. With each response, we stuck in a pin to identify the location and the world seemed to shrink. We weren't just suburban kids whose world was measured in city blocks. We suddenly had contacts in Japan, Geneva, India.

One of WE Charity's first actions was a petition to free child rights advocate Kailash Satyarthi, who would go on to win the Nobel Peace Prize 20 years later. At the time, he was a little-known activist repeatedly detained by India's government for his incendiary work kicking down doors to free children. Ours was a pre-Internet petition, so we collected signatures the old-fashioned way, visiting malls and farmers' markets to gather 3,000 handwritten names, which we mailed to Indian government officials in a shoebox. When Kailash was released, he told us that the idea of children rallying to his defense was the most heartwarming action taken on his behalf during his time of turmoil. He invited me to visit him, halfway around the world.

Back home, kids my own age seemed skeptical of the small geographic sphere in which I operated. When I spoke to school groups, which I often did, other students would ask if I'd ever met any child laborers, if I'd ever seen the problem I was asking them to help solve. I had to admit that I hadn't. I started to look at our map differently—less like a collection of flat, colorful shapes and more like an invitation.

When WE Charity was just a few months old, we received our first major donation. After a speech I'd given at the Ontario Federation of Labour convention, delegates stood up, one by one, each pledging thousands of dollars. It was like a bidding war, except that every contribution counted—for a total of C$150,000. We were shocked and humbled by the support. We knew this was a sum that could really change lives. I knew I had to find out how to invest it to achieve the greatest impact. I needed to meet working children, speak with them, and bear witness to the problem we had already devoted so much time and money to support. I decided to visit Southeast Asia, with stops in Bangladesh, Pakistan and India. It might seem ludicrous today for a 12-year-old to plan that trip, and in some sense it was—I went to Asia before I was allowed to take the Toronto subway by myself. But in another sense, a much more powerful one, it was essential. It's hard to describe how it felt at the time, all these years later. Something compelled me, from the pit of my stomach, to meet the children I'd been thinking of for months. It was a feeling unlike anything I've ever experienced. That trip would change my life, as well as the lives of millions of others.

The weeks leading up to my departure were a bit of a blur. I wrote to UNICEF's regional partners and other local organizations to help build an itinerary (many didn't realize they were talking to a 12-year-old kid until I arrived). I was very fortunate to find a suitable chaperone in a family friend, Alam Rahman, who would meet me on our first stop in Dhaka, Bangladesh.

There are too many stories to tell here. We met Mother Teresa at her mission house in Calcutta, where I asked her to pray for child laborers. In Pakistan, we visited Iqbal Masih's mother and sister in Lahore and paid our respects at his grave in his home village of Muridke. We heard the family's stories about the boy who broke free from bonded labor and spoke out against his captors, but who also loved to cook and play with his sister. In India, I was involved in my first factory raid to rescue child slaves and return them to their parents; there we would eventually start the first real chapter of WE Charity's international development work.

Unfolding the map

Raids were conducted like covert military operations. Locations weren't revealed until moments before departure, lest the plan to rescue child slaves should leak to factory owners with more to gain from imprisoned children than free ones. Only a few leaders at the organizations we'd connected with knew details. Fortunately, we were in contact with Kailash, who by then had been released from detention. Midway into the trip, while Alam and I were in Varanasi, India, we got word from Kailash of a planned carpet factory raid just a few hours away from where we were staying. We were to meet him at the home of one of the local agents who worked for the rights group he'd partnered with.

Over the years, WE Charity's work in India has been focused in the states of West Bengal and Tamil Nadu. Now the charity works in Rajasthan to bring quality education to children where rates of illiteracy, child labor and child marriage are high.

We took a taxi to the address Kailash had given us. We knocked on the back door of a small shop. A man answered and looked us over, then beyond us into the alleyway. "Was there anybody with you? You're certain you weren't followed?" Secrecy was paramount.

The team piled into two Jeeps. A BBC reporter was filming, and Alam shot his own footage.

The factory was a single-story structure in the middle of a clearing. As police broke through the trees, their guns in view, the team rushed through the open doors of the factory.

They didn't find the owner. Somehow he'd been tipped off and fled before we arrived. But 22 children were rescued that day, most between the ages of eight and twelve. Many suffered from the lack of ventilation inside the factory, with its dirt floors and shuttered windows. Wool dust had collected in their lungs. Coughs broke their raspy breathing. Skin infections had been left untreated. Their hands were callused and pitted from the incessant tying of knots.

"I fell asleep at the loom," one boy said. He pushed aside his hair to show a scar left by a gash on his neck, his punishment for sleeping.

I joined the team to reunite the boys with their families. We left early the next morning, 30 of us piling into two Jeeps to begin the 11-hour trip to the boys' village.

We hadn't gone far when one of the boys started to sing. The others quickly joined in, their voices soaring above the noise, their hands clapping a steady rhythm. Even Alam picked up on the words and chanted along.

"Free!" was the Hindi word they sang. "We are free! Free!"

Next to me sat Ramatha, and on his lap sat eight-year-old Munnilal, who wore an old pink tank top, full of holes, and a pair of plaid pants too big for his small frame. I asked Munnilal if he'd ever been to school, and with Kailash as translator, he explained he had. His parents couldn't read or write but wanted their son to learn. One day,

a man turned up in their village and told his parents that their son could stay in school part-time while earning money weaving carpets. Munnilal could study *and* support the family. It seemed almost too good to be true, so they accepted the offer. Munnilal told me he was given no money and hadn't seen his family since.

On the long ride, Munnilal was one of the last children we returned home; it was dark by the time we reached his village. His father answered the door and stood stunned for a moment before shouting back into the house for the rest of the family to wake up. His mother was the last one to appear from inside, behind his grandparents and younger sister. She stood staring at her boy before managing to whisper, "Munnilal, can it really be you?" In her arms she cradled a baby boy, a brother Munnilal had never met. The family offered us what food they had—tea and plain biscuits—while Munnilal's mother kept repeating that her son had grown so thin. They were full of emotion, the anger at being cheated and the joy and disbelief at their son's return. I said a tearful goodbye to my new friend.

Munnilal and those children are the reason I went to India. I still count the journey to return them home among the most seminal moments of my life, though now with renewed perspective. I didn't realize it then, but the boys weren't really free. They were free from immediate harm and their master's cruelty, but what did their futures hold? Our first significant project was to help fund a rescue home, Bal Ashram, built for these kids and other freed child slaves.

If you read this book's introduction, you know that this story had an imperfect ending. We quickly learned that children need to be free from poverty, not just factories. We saw that some organizations would "rescue" the same children again and again, and each time they were sold back into slavery. Their parents were poor and desperate, taking money in exchange for their own children in order to survive. Bringing their kids back didn't solve their problems. One of our greatest advantages in starting when we were so young was that we were quick to acknowledge that we didn't have the answers, and thus sought to ask questions and learn from the local community. As teenagers, we sat under trees and within mud-walled homes to be schooled by the greatest experts on international development: the local community members. Our learnings about the complexity of development shaped WE Charity's international model and its five pillars that work in tandem. Grounded in local knowledge and backed by some of the world's foremost research institutes on impact measurement and evaluation, our WE Village model offers education, clean water, health care, food security and alternative income programming in India and other countries.

Over the years we've worked in West Bengal and Tamil Nadu, and are now focused in Rajasthan, a region with high rates of child labor, poverty and incidents of child marriage. One-third of the population is tribal, and even more marginalized. The country's Scheduled Tribes (Indigenous peoples) and Scheduled Castes (Dalits, or "untouchables") have very few of the opportunities and resources available to upper castes in the religious and social hierarchy that dates back centuries. Nearly all of our community partners are members of tribal groups who have limited capacity to benefit from government and development programs, and as a result have little access to schooling, clean water, health care or sufficient means of income.

Many of WE Charity's partners are smallholder farmers in regions with few other job prospects. The organization's agricultural training programs teach best practices for irrigation, crop spacing and seed variety. Participating farmers have more than doubled their crop yields.

In one of the poorest countries in the world, Rajasthan is among its poorest regions, a desert state with few employment prospects. Many of our community partners are smallholder farmers. Although the province is the country's largest in terms of land mass, it has only a fraction of its groundwater. Agricultural work is difficult to sustain, especially through the dry seasons. WE Charity's country team works with local farmers on seed selection, irrigation, well rehabilitation and capacity building. The impact has been incredible to witness. With rehabilitated wells, acreage increases as irrigation reaches more land. Improved crop health and variety has more than doubled crop yields for most farmers. Noja Bhil, whom you'll meet here, increased his wheat crop production by 50 percent over his previous harvests and saw a 173 percent increase in his corn harvest.

Rajasthan has the country's lowest female literacy rate. Young tribal girls are especially prone to discrimination, receiving lower wages at work and given smaller portions of food at home, a sacrifice for their fathers and brothers, who eat more. They are much less likely than their brothers to go to school. But our education and water pillars are bringing girls back to class. At Kalthana Primary School, WE rebuilt classrooms and installed latrines with handwashing stations. Girls are most likely to drop out after they hit puberty—lacking private washroom facilities at school, they simply don't show up. Our toilets have increased attendance rates, with girls staying in class to study and grow into strong leaders.

For parents, especially mothers of daughters, WE increases income prospects with our opportunity pillar and a local breed of "super goat." The animal matures more quickly and yields more offspring and more milk, making it a smart investment. Community-led women's groups breed and sell the goats, increasing local household incomes and giving parents the resources to send their daughters—and sons—to school. You'll read more about our super goats here, and the women entrepreneurs who are now running small businesses.

You'll also meet Mulki Bhil, one of our health mobilizers, who walks for miles every day in search of new and expectant mothers in a province with high maternal mortality rates. After WE Charity refurbished her community's *anganwadi*, a health center and preschool that offers free pre- and postnatal care, Mulki Bhil set out to give mothers and their babies a better chance at a healthy start. There are so many others on the ground, too many to mention here, working on every aspect of our five-pillar model.

I've since been back to India more times than I can count, bringing youth, families and donors on ME to WE Trips to visit and volunteer on our projects. Sometimes I think about the first children who were rescued in 1995. Thankfully, today we are working to ensure other children never experience that same fate, and they are forever freed from exploitation by the capacity to gain access to education, to build capacity in their own communities and to lift themselves and their families from poverty.

Impact at a glance

Focus on Rajasthan

Population: 69 million
Languages: Hindi is the most commonly spoken national language. English is also officially recognized and there are 22 state languages in addition to regional dialects. Mewari is the most commonly spoken dialect where WE Charity works in India.
Population with secondary education: 25%
Literacy rate: 81% male and 53% female.
Rajasthan has the lowest literacy rate for women in India.
Children under five affected by stunting: 39%
Rural households with clean drinking water on the premises: 40%
Infant mortality ratio: 47 per 1,000 live births (one of the highest in India)

**The above statistics are drawn from the World Bank, CIA World Factbook and local government sources.

Despite impressive gains in economic investment and output, India still faces significant issues such as overpopulation, environmental degradation, extensive poverty and ethnic and religious strife. WE Charity initially worked in West Bengal and Tamil Nadu and now operates in the desert state of Rajasthan in northwest India, which has one of the largest tribal populations in the country, as well as a significant number of Dalits, the caste formerly known as "untouchables." The social and economic marginalization they face has resulted in rates of illiteracy and malnutrition higher than the national average, and even more so among women and girls. While Rajasthan has five percent of India's population, it has only one percent of its water resources, which hobbles farmers struggling to provide for their families.

WE Charity partners with remote villages in Rajasthan's Mewar region to implement its five-pillar model for sustainable development. Through consultation and collective action, communities forge solutions to improve quality of life for their families and for future generations.

Impact by the numbers by 2020

⭐ EDUCATION

100+ schoolrooms built, including classrooms, teacher offices and libraries

💧 WATER

20 water systems built or rehabilitated, including hand pumps installed at schools and wells deepened to improve irrigation

❤️ HEALTH

11,700+ catchment area served by seven rehabilitated maternal health centers (*anganwadis*)

700+ new stoves and chimneys (smokeless *chullah*s) installed in family homes

🌾 FOOD

200+ farmers participating in food programming, improving subsistence farming yields and cash crop production

⚲ OPPORTUNITY

20+ women's savings groups established

600+ "super" goats distributed, providing women with a sustainable source of income

Super goats send kids to school

In rural Rajasthan, a women's group learns to raise goats as a reliable source of income so they no longer have to depend on their children's labor.

It's grass-cutting season in the village of Kamoda, and for Kesi Bhil, every moment of daylight is money.

At the homestead we find only Rekha, Kesi's 14-year-old daughter. She is perched on the terrace wall, skinny legs clad in pink tights. Her twin braids are tied with brown ribbons, the last hint of the day's school uniform. She shields an open book from the late-afternoon glare and tells us her mother won't be back for hours.

Kesi is out gathering hay for the animals and, possibly, to sell to wealthier farmers—if she collects enough. She'll work until she can barely see the scythe's curved blade in front of her. In earlier years, the whole family would be hip-deep in the field alongside her, the younger children grazing goats while the older ones cut the long grass at the roots. For the residents of Kamoda—a cluster of hamlets in the foothills of the Aravalli Mountains—subsistence was once a family affair.

The sky is a deep lilac when finally we spot Kesi turning into this network of powdery mud houses. Thin and wiry and wrapped in a magenta sari, she looks more like a teenaged girl than a 37-year-old mother of six. She smiles briefly, revealing perfect white teeth, then scoops water from a bowl to splash her face before joining us in her doorway.

This evening, she has a quiet strength about her, even after a full day of physical labor. According to WE Charity's records, this wasn't always the case. Kesi and her children once suffered from ill health and malnutrition, surviving almost entirely on plain wheat roti. Every workday, she recalls, began with only a tumbler of black tea.

As Kesi speaks, a young goat creeps along the terrace wall and butts its head softly against her shoulder. She pulls the kid into her lap affectionately.

PILLARS

 OPPORTUNITY

 EDUCATION

Kesi Bhil: mother, businesswoman and goat breeder

Kesi's daily routine has long included fetching water from the village well, gathering hay for her livestock and preparing food for her children. When her community partnered with WE Charity, she embarked on a series of subtle yet significant changes. Kesi learned to boil the water she collected, eliminating parasites and halting the cycle of illness that once plagued her family. She replaced her stove with a new model supplied by WE Charity to funnel smoke out of the house, reducing respiratory infections. And with beans and lentils grown right at home, she boosted her children's protein intake. By introducing simple practices, Kesi saw a dramatic improvement in her family's quality of life. And as the community partnership deepened, she learned that the best was yet to come.

Kamoda's self-help group is born

In 2011, WE Charity's work in Kamoda began with basic surveys. Of 850 village residents, roughly one-third belonged to a Scheduled Tribe—a government designation recognizing historically marginalized Indigenous communities, often the oldest inhabitants of the land. Isolated amidst rugged terrain, these groups have been able to preserve their cultural heritage but have largely been excluded from development processes and access to basic resources and opportunities.

WE Charity needs assessments revealed that only 40 percent of Kamoda's children were enrolled at the local primary school. The battered walls and roof of the school's two classrooms offered little shelter during the monsoon season, though flooded floors and decay weren't the only deterrents. In the weathered hills of this region, where tomorrow's meal is dependent on today's work, few parents could do without their children's contribution to the family income. Like other women in her small hamlet, Kesi taught her children to do the hard work needed to survive.

In this context, baby steps often work best. WE Charity's team, headed by micro-credit expert Manish Sharma, mobilized 10 women in Kamoda to come together as a *swayam sahayata samuh*, or self-help group. Though they lived in the same settlement and shared resources as a matter of principle, the new group took on a formal goal: equipping members to generate a reliable source of income—without having to rely on their children's labor. This last point was crucial. In order to join the group and reap the benefits, members had to pledge to send their children to school.

Kesi was not keen. Her eldest son, Ambu, was already in school, but she needed her daughter Rekha, then eight years old, to help care for her three younger siblings and manage daily chores.

This is where the power of the collective did its work. Women who were committed to the program motivated the skeptics to take part. They understood that as members of the group, they were responsible not only for their own but for all of the hamlet's children. They also recognized the broader changes unfolding in their community.

WE Charity had started renovations at Kamoda Primary, a government school built decades earlier. For the first time, children would be able to study seated at desks, and teachers would be equipped with adequate supplies. Plans were also underway for the construction of an additional classroom to accommodate an influx of new students. Washbasins and latrines would follow, drawing from the village well that was soon to be deepened. After much convincing by her peers, Kesi relented and enrolled Rekha in Grade 1.

ABOVE: *Kamoda's self-help group was founded to help women generate a new and sustainable source of income and save for the future. WE Charity supports them with business capital, such as goats, for microenterprises and training in skills like animal husbandry and financial literacy.*
FACING PAGE: *For Kesi and her sisters-in-law, pooling resources was once a means of survival. But with the formation of the women's self-help group, it is now an investment in new opportunities.*

FACING PAGE: *In order to join the women's self-help group and reap the financial benefits, Kesi had to agree to enroll her children in school. The earnings from her new small business would replace the contributions her children had previously made to the family income.*
TOP RIGHT: *Kesi's fourth child, Panki*
BOTTOM LEFT AND RIGHT: *Kesi's daughter Rekha*

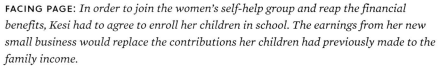

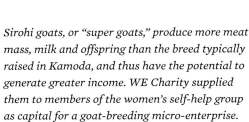

Sirohi goats, or "super goats," produce more meat mass, milk and offspring than the breed typically raised in Kamoda, and thus have the potential to generate greater income. WE Charity supplied them to members of the women's self-help group as capital for a goat-breeding micro-enterprise.

Introducing the super goats

A concrete incentive for joining the group was the promise of business capital—and in rural Rajasthan, that means goats. Goat rearing wasn't new to these women, most of whom were smallholder farmers whose families had kept goats for generations. Kesi herself had two at the time, though she considered them less an asset than a burden. The local mixed-breed goats produce little milk and easily succumb to illness, but these were not the goats being proffered.

Rather, Manish and team spoke of "super goats," more formally known as Sirohi goats, named for the Rajasthani district from which they originate. This breed typically produces twice as much milk as the local variety, reproduces more rapidly, grows larger and proves resilient even in poor conditions. WE Charity would entrust five female super goats to each of the group members, with one or two male bucks to be shared among them. Through a series of trainings with subject-matter experts, the women would learn how to properly care for the animals and maintain their health through immunizations, deworming and the provision of clean, safe shelter. They would also learn how to breed and sell them, creating a stable and significant source of income.

As part of their training, the women were tasked with building proper goat sheds; the mesh and cement were provided by WE Charity. Though Kesi had kept goats throughout her married life, she had never had the means to protect them from predators, except to bring them into the tiny one-room hut her family shared with her husband's parents and siblings. The two goats slept alongside her children, husband and in-laws, as well as all of their worldly possessions. But once the cement was dry on the new shed, Kesi and her kin would have the house to themselves.

WE Charity's opportunity pillar programs in India are designed to support women's empowerment. An increase in women's income not only results in greater access to nutritious foods and education for their children, it also gives women a greater voice in household decision-making.

Bringing home the herd

The goat-buying trip remains a historic event in the lives of Kamoda's women. They set out in two rented vans and stopped at a roadside restaurant for lunch—a luxury no one had previously experienced. They also traveled farther than ever before, to the city of Devgarh, 75 miles away. Few in the group had gone more than three miles from home before. One or two might have been to Udaipur, famously known as the "city of lakes," but then only for treatment of a medical emergency. In preparation, the women consulted with the village priest to find an auspicious day for the journey.

In their minds, and the minds of their men, the self-help group members were also defying expectations. On hearing plans for the excursion, some of Kamoda's husbands formed an oddly unsupportive union. What did their wives know about choosing goats? Even now, years later, Manish recalls the group's focused energy: "In other communities, a women needs her husband's company to go out. But in Kamoda, the women were motivated and ready to go. They wanted to choose their goats."

Rekha, Kesi's daughter, grazes her family's "super goat" at the end of the school day.

WE Charity's team had rallied the Sirohi goat breeders of Devgarh to create a small marketplace for the visit. Accompanied by a veterinarian from Udaipur, who assisted in choosing healthy animals, the women picked their way through the herds, boldly examining udders, checking teeth. Each woman carried her own marker—bright strips of sari or thread brought from home—to identify the goats that met her criteria. For Kesi, two features were paramount: "The goat should be healthy, and it should not be thin."

The women struggled to select goats in Devgarh, not because—as their husbands feared—they didn't know what they were doing, but because their standards were too high. By early evening, when they should have been heading home, each woman was one goat short of the five-goat quota. Having come such a long way, they were unwilling to accept less than perfect animals. Manish and the veterinarian set about the village, hastily wrangling more goats for consideration. So, when the group traveled back in the darkness, each woman had precisely what she had come for—a solid base for a new home business.

From clay pot to bank account

When the breeding and sale of super goats first began yielding profits, Kamoda's self-help group morphed into a savings collective. In monthly meetings, each member put 200 rupees (US$2.88) into a clay pot that was kept safely by their elected treasurer. A WE Charity facilitator noted contributions in the self-help group's ledger, a blue volume of graph paper. Minutes were read aloud and confirmed by the women's thumbprints in lieu of their signatures, as none were literate at that time. The practice of saving was new to Kesi, who quickly discovered that siphoning even a small amount meant less money for daily expenses. At the same time, there was comfort in knowing the collection would be available to any group member in case of emergency. They were building something that had never existed before: a safety net.

Over time, the group itself became a source of strength and security. Meetings were an occasion for continued training with WE Charity staff, not only on potential uses for monthly savings but also on simple ways to improve the health and well-being of their families. As women shared experiences of frequent illness and hunger, they also explored the merits of boiling water and proper handwashing, and starting kitchen gardens to bolster nutrition. They were introduced to smokeless *chullah*s, or chimneys, which funnel cooking smoke out of the house, reducing the incidence of respiratory illness. With WE Charity's help, each woman had one installed in her home.

Six months into saving, it was time to graduate to a group bank account. Keeping the clay pot at home was admittedly risky, but for those denied the luxury of education, entering a financial institution was equally unnerving. Manish's team facilitated introductions with the local bank manager to create a sense of comfort with the process. Group members also opened personal accounts and began signing off on new deposits with every goat sale. In this way, the animals became a pension plan for the women of Kamoda village, each goat possessing a store of value.

With respect to the group account, several investment ideas have been put up for consideration and some funds set aside specifically for goat health—to keep up with deworming and vaccinations for growing numbers. While WE Charity has already rehabilitated the village well to allow for greater water security, the women are contemplating taking the next step on their own—installing a pump that will lift water from the well, creating access to greater depths in drier months. Occasionally they also tease Manish, vowing to spend all their savings on a big picnic.

Every month, members of Kamoda's self-help group contribute to a collective savings pot. At first the women stored their money in a clay pot, but in time they graduated to a group bank account.

Signs of change

In the initial days after the birth of a new kid, Kesi tends to the mother goat the way she would care for a human mother. She cleans her bed thoroughly, melts blocks of yellow cane sugar, known as jaggery, in hot water for her to drink and provides extra food to help her produce enough milk and build strength. She also ties a black thread around the baby's neck, just as she once marked her own newborns' cheeks with *kohl*, to ward off negative energy.

This tenderness and superstition coexist with the practical mindset of a business-woman. Presenting the latest addition to her family, born just a few days earlier, Kesi says starkly: "Yes, we are happy about it. But we would be happier if it were a male buck, because it would be worth more." Still, she submits that a female goat is valuable for its ability to produce milk and kids.

We ask how many goats have been born to the household, which sparks debate between Kesi and her husband, Jetha, who has returned from excavating rocks in the hills. He claims ten, and she counters that only three are left—the rest have been sold. It seems our translator has lost the thread. Whatever the number, it's clear they don't want to disclose it, out of modesty or perhaps fear that their good fortune will arouse envy. Like everyone in this hamlet, though, Kesi and her husband are working harder than ever before.

"We don't ask the children to do anything," Kesi says, explaining that all but her youngest—three-year-old Prakash—are in school. "They are focused on their studies and we don't want to disturb them." She and Jetha have taken over the household chores. Neither had any education growing up, so the only work available to them is physical labor. They don't want their children to face the same limitations.

Their daughter Rekha is in Grade 6. Jetha hopes she will be able to get a good job in the hotels cropping up throughout the region. "We don't know what she wants to become," he says, "but we'll do everything to make sure she gets what she wants." For Kesi and her husband, skepticism has given way to deep investment in the promise of education. This means a commitment to saving for their children's future studies.

Kesi may be hesitant to talk about the changes in her life, but the signs are all around. Once we leave her to the evening routine, she will begin her last task of the day: sitting down to practice her own signature under Rekha's careful guidance. When it's time to retire, she will herd the children not into her in-laws' hut but rather into a room of their own—a sturdy concrete construction built with the proceeds of her goat sales. And in the morning, before all the chores begin, Kesi will brew tea thick with milk. She works hard for every drop.

DEEPA SHANKARAN

For Kesi and her husband, skepticism has given way to deep investment in the promise of education.

TOP LEFT: *Kesi's husband, Jetha, with niece Varsha (center) and son Prakash (right)*

TOP RIGHT AND BOTTOM LEFT: *Like most of the women in her community, Kesi never had the opportunity to go to school. But with the help of a WE Charity mobilizer, she is learning to write her name.*

A godmother makes a wish for education

PILLARS: EDUCATION, HEALTH, OPPORTUNITY

Mohani Bhil comes from a long line of priests, advisors and healers and is known to have special powers—most notably, the power of persuasion. While she has no children, she is considered a godmother to the girls and boys of her hamlet in Kamoda village, and has long foreseen the potential of education to transform their future. She only needed a partner to help realize the vision.

Previously, Mohani was the one and only woman from her hamlet elected to the village council. In that role, she scouted opportunities for her community to leverage. During her tenure, the government funded the construction of latrines in Kamoda, but the pits were dug and then ignored, as people were used to their own ways. Real change would require real investment.

When she encountered WE Charity at the site of a proposed new school, she served as a guide, a bridge and a backer, persuading families to enroll their children. She said the school was concrete proof of a changing landscape, which couldn't be denied.

This was WE's first venture with Mohani Bhil, but hardly the last. For every imagined project in Kamoda, the organization seeks her blessing and influence as someone with the power to see what is possible.

DEEPA SHANKARAN

Mohani is a trusted leader and advisor in the village of Kamoda, and an early adopter of WE Charity development initiatives. Forward-looking and open to possibilities, she is consistently the first to embrace new opportunities and motivate her community to do the same.

Teaching the language of opportunity

A veteran activist for girls' education teams up with WE Charity mobilizers to ensure every child in her community has the chance to go to school.

If you are a girl from Kalthana village in the hills of rural Rajsamand, and you've managed to get to school, chances are you didn't make the journey alone. Jummi Bhil—teacher, taskmaster, activist—fights for every student under her watch. Working alongside WE Charity mobilizers who travel door-to-door, she is determined to shift the mindset on education.

Jummi is well versed in the case against sending girls to school. With few employment opportunities in the countryside, most parents prefer to bet on their sons. Daughters are considered risky investments, so their opportunities, even their portions of food, are rationed accordingly. A girl's time is thought better spent looking after the household and preparing for married life. These arguments are familiar to Jummi, who was ridiculed for being the only girl in her village to go to school. Oddly enough, it was she who was desperate to drop out and her father who insisted she be educated.

"At night, I would make up my mind not to go to school the next day because people were saying so many things," she says. "But in the morning, my father would call me to get ready."

To toughen her against her critics, he took Jummi to the city to see women in different lines of skilled work and urged her to start planning her future. Her earliest dreams were practical. "I understood that if I completed my education, I could eat well and have good clothing."

She went on to secondary school in a neighboring village, a grueling three-mile hike through the forest each way. Such efforts build strength. By the time Jummi completed her studies, she was devoted to nurturing the dreams of other girls.

As a teacher at Kalthana Primary, a government school that WE Charity has supported since 2013, she is a bridge between past and future. "Everyone knows Jummi Bhil. She has been working here for a long time," says Hiranshi Bhatnagar, a WE Charity mobilizer, who explains that progress begins with local leaders like Jummi showing the way.

Jummi Bhil: teacher, mentor and advocate for girls' education

At the start of the academic year, Jummi and two WE Charity fieldworkers visit the home of every child in the village, girls and boys alike. This march goes on for 15 to 20 days. A loudspeaker attached to the roof of the organization's vehicle plays a lively message, drumming up excitement about the start of school and sharing news of any improvements to the facilities. New classrooms, new latrines, proper desks and chairs! A computer lab! While this last feature may not be widely understood, it is a symbol of advancement and opportunity.

In this rural landscape, a vehicle can only take you so far. Jummi leads the team on foot from hamlet to hamlet. Sometimes they are persuading parents to enroll the children that have just come of age. More often they are reminding them to send the older ones back to school. Over the holidays, parents grow accustomed to having their children work at home—collecting water, grazing livestock, plowing the fields—the daily burden is lighter when it is shared. Jummi speaks their language, but she also speaks of possibilities. She helps them see that education can bring the long-term security they seek.

"Change is coming," says Hiranshi, citing the government's commitment to ensuring free and compulsory primary education, as well as the burgeoning tourism industry and job market in this part of the state. "Still, we need to go door-to-door."

As a teacher, Jummi monitors student attendance and follows up with parents to ensure that every child in her community has the chance to go to school.

"I was 14 when the proposals started coming. If not for Madam Jummi, I'd be living with my in-laws instead of at school," says Jamuna.

Solidarity between Jummi and WE Charity is effective where separate efforts would fall short. "Those who don't listen to her will listen to us, because they know the work that WE Charity is doing in the community," says Hiranshi. "And without Madam Jummi, we are incomplete."

Jamuna Bhil, 16 and in Grade 9, says she owes every year of her studies to Jummi, who first convinced her mother to enroll her in school. Jummi gave her the books and school supplies she couldn't afford and persuaded her mother year after year to put off Jamuna's marriage until she had graduated. "I was 14 when the proposals started coming. If not for Madam Jummi, I'd be living with my in-laws instead of at school," says Jamuna, adding that her teacher is an inspiration to many girls in the village.

"It gives me immense pleasure to be a role model," says Jummi. "At the same time, I know people talk about me. They say I should be at home like other women. l let it go in one ear and out the other. I know the importance of what I am doing."

DEEPA SHANKARAN

LEFT: *Jamuna (left) stands with her mother, Gomali*

BELOW LEFT: *Jummi was Jamuna's teacher, but also her champion, encouraging Jamuna to focus on her studies and convincing her mother to delay Jamuna's marriage until after she had completed secondary school.*

BELOW RIGHT: *Jamuna (center) and friends*

The best toilets in town

PILLARS: EDUCATION, HEALTH AND WATER

A girls' washroom can be a refuge, a gathering place, the site of discovery for first periods. That is, if your bathrooms hide behind closed doors and running water is standard issue. For girls in rural India, the trip to relieve themselves can be so humiliating that it disrupts studies and threatens futures.

At Kalthana Primary School in Rajasthan, the open-air toilet block was a set of holes in the concrete floor separated by partitions, like urinal stalls. Only the boys dared use it. Girls walked into the nearby field, far enough from the property for privacy, missing significant portions of class. Others dropped out entirely once they started menstruating.

All that stood between these girls and a proper education was a minor feat of engineering.

In 2015, WE Charity hired a plumber to rejig the school's hand pump, the lever that draws clean water up from a borehole. The same system can now divert flow to an underground pipe that feeds a storage tank atop the school's roof, where gravity's downward pull makes history. Kalthana's primary school is the region's first property with running water.

New plumbing allowed for flush toilets in a newly built washroom block, with separate facilities for boys and girls, doors with locks, and a handwashing station with a row of shiny faucets. The flush toilets brought privacy, sanitation and desks filled with girls.

Over in a neighboring village at Verdara Senior Secondary School, the call of nature is more compromising for older girls with changing bodies. Verdara is the destination for Kalthana's graduates, should they make it this far. Dropouts shoot up after puberty and the start of menstruation; girls can miss a full week of lessons to avoid a hike to the bushes out back.

That was before. Now, Verdara's crowning glory is a long steel sink with faucets protruding at intervals, a communal handwashing station that runs the length of both the girls' and boys' facilities, with flush toilets built by WE Charity. Student attendance and retention are up.

Solving toilet troubles helps stop cycles of illiteracy, early marriage and teen pregnancy. Classrooms are essential, but so is the girls' bathroom.

KATIE HEWITT

ABOVE: *Twins Geeta and Seeta Kanwar show off the new girls' washroom at Verdara Senior Secondary School.*

BELOW AND FACING PAGE: *Students at Kalthana Primary use the hand pump and handwashing station outside the school's newly built washroom block.*

A wish and a well

Technology and blind faith help bring WE Charity's water pillar to smallholder farmers in a desert province in India.

The sky is almost cartoonishly blue, an innocent disguise hiding the power it holds over the man underneath. Kharta Bhil is perched on the lip of a well, a circle of stones that rises from the belly of the earth to just above the grass. At 85, his hands are etched like the deep, rough lines of tree bark, and he has the stoic countenance of a man resigned to his fate.

Kharta is the fifth generation to farm here in the rural Rajasthani village of Verdara, where he helped his father dig the well by hand as a boy. After decades of flooding fields for irrigation, the well ran dry. Kharta's farm and the plots of a dozen other farmers who share the water source were in distress. Crops failed. Food was scarce.

When WE Charity got word, two local team members arrived with a rather intimidating solution. It involved exploding dynamite and heavy machinery to haul out the well's insides. A kind of controlled destruction would break new water veins in the rock, WE's development experts promised, to increase depth and the water's recharge rate.

"*Kisan darap riya ha*," Kharta remembers, speaking in Mewari. "The farmers were afraid."

Their well had once filled up over the rainy season, with enough water to last all year. Lately the rains had become unpredictable. By summer's dry season, the water was often gone. Kharta and the others faced a choice: rely on the rain and watch the well deplete with the changing seasons, or call in the machines and blow up their very means of survival in the hopes of coaxing out more water. Both options seemed like a gamble.

This is the story of an old man versus nature.

As benefactors go, Mother Nature can seem largely indifferent. Rajasthan has 10 percent of India's land mass, but only 1.1 percent of the country's surface water. It's a desert state of extremes, where monsoon rains abruptly flood fields after summer's dry heat. Residents are almost completely dependent on wells that draw water from the earth when it doesn't fall from the sky. If that groundwater isn't replenished fast enough, farmers like Kharta suffer.

PILLARS

⬥ WATER

⬥ FOOD

Kharta Bhil: risk-taker, mobilizer and local hero

Seventy years ago, when Kharta was 15, his father, grandfather and farmers from a dozen other nearby plots set out in search of a spot to dig. Without a bedrock assessment or a geological map, they looked to the ridges in the nearby hills where the rains slid down like a slalom course. At the bottom, they found a low-lying patch where groundwater often pooled. That would be the place.

A dozen men hacked at soil and rock with crowbars, shovels, chisels and hammers, breaking stone by hand for six hours every day, hauling it out with oxen. A teenage Kharta joined them. There was no school in the village at the time, Kharta adds through a translator, so he was free to work. The group only stopped during monsoon season, when their hole filled up with rain. Then they went to temple and prayed the water would last through the dry season.

The men dug like that for a year, enough for a continual supply of groundwater that would irrigate their surrounding land. They planted corn in the summer (the *kharif* crop) and wheat in the winter (the *rabi* crop). Their prayers had been answered—sort of. Summer after summer came, and the water level slowly dropped.

Wheat is a thirsty crop, Kharta explains. From planting to harvest, in this climate and with this crop variety, fields must be irrigated six or seven times over the season. Every time, the soil sucks up nearly 40,000 gallons of water—per plot. Kharta's crop alone would drink about 265,000 gallons every season. Their hand-dug well was regenerating only 8,000 gallons per day. So it became a math problem.

The farmers had to ration: whose land would be watered first, and how many times? Who planted first? Whose fields are farthest from the source? How can we crunch the numbers so we can all feed our families? Water levels kept shrinking, and the farmers reached a point when they couldn't manage.

ABOVE: *Seventy years ago, Kharta helped his father dig this well by hand. But as an elderly man, he watched the well go dry during summer months. When crops failed, he agreed to let WE Charity blast out the well to make water more plentiful.*

FACING PAGE: *With an increase in the recharge rate of the refurbished well, Kharta's crops are flourishing from year-round irrigation.*

Not every well can be rehabilitated. Only the right kind of rock and sediment will support a narrow tunnel and the pressure of holding thousands of gallons of water. Before approaching farmers, WE Charity conducts hydrological surveys to determine viability, ensuring that the well won't collapse in on itself when it's deepened and that it will, in fact, release more water. Only about one in every 15 wells assessed in this region is selected.

When Kharta's well was chosen, he reluctantly agreed. WE Charity would bring in equipment, hire machine operators and fund the project. All 15 farmers had to consent, and they had to help with manual labor, under the reasoning that community buy-in

ensures long-term sustainability. It required Kharta to convince 14 other famers that dynamite was a viable option. Most of the men had never been to school and couldn't read an assessment report. What proof did they have that this would work?

"We're not able to do any farming," Kharta told the non-believers, "so let's try and see."

The crane had to be shipped in, piece by piece, over narrow footpaths and assembled on-site. Dynamite loosened the large rocks so that smaller pieces could be broken up by hand, this time easily lifted out by the crane. Explosions were set off at night, when the surrounding hills went quiet and there was less chance of foot traffic. After an initial drilling, experts coached the locals to dig this way and that, angling to hit deeper and deeper water veins in the rocks.

Kharta watched as the well was temporarily destroyed, its guts stacked up into neat piles. "Even when the work was half completed, I didn't have faith," he admits. "But I was not sharing my worry with anyone."

Kharta and his ancestors spent a year digging 100 feet into the ground. This time, the same task took two months, increasing the depth to 200 feet. Rehabilitation also included masonry lining to keep the water contained, and a parapet was added—the stone lip around the well—to keep out runoff waste from neighboring livestock.

Water capacity and recharge rate increased almost immediately. Crop yields grew and a whole new planting season was added. Green gram, a kind of bean, now grows in the peak of summer, an additional crop that thrives at a time without rain, when no planting had been possible.

The refurbished well has a water recharge rate of 21,000 gallons a day, widening the farmers' scope of arable land to 227,010 square feet from 52,097. Kharta's plot alone is now 27,000 square feet, up from 7,000. The effect on his family is immeasurable. "My family has enough food, and we are healthy. Whatever we want to grow, we can grow."

Since rehab, the well has never run dry, even in the summer.

Kharta has two grown sons, who have been helping him in the fields for some time. One day they will take over the land. Kharta's four grandsons will inherit it after that, and his great-grandchildren after that. "I rest more than I used to," Kharta says.

KATIE HEWITT

"My family has enough food, and we are healthy. Whatever we want to grow, we can grow," says Kharta. Since rehab, the well has never run dry, even in the summer.

For his part in bringing water back to the village, Kharta has become a local hero.

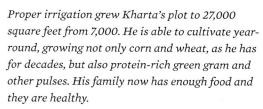

Proper irrigation grew Kharta's plot to 27,000 square feet from 7,000. He is able to cultivate year-round, growing not only corn and wheat, as he has for decades, but also protein-rich green gram and other pulses. His family now has enough food and they are healthy.

Hope on the hills

One woman takes on the challenges, hopes and fears of new mothers in Rajasthan's remote mountains.

Mulki Bhil spends her days walking in search of expectant mothers. She walks over hills and through wheat fields, in the blistering heat of summer and in spring's monsoon rains.

PILLAR

♥ HEALTH

She works at the *anganwadi*, a health center and refuge for maternal care in her village of Kalthana, which offers free checkups, immunizations, nutrient packets and preschool for children until age six. On paper, the anganwadi seems like a mecca for the kind of social services that many Western nations can't achieve. But for Mulki, whose job is recruitment, it can be a hard sell. The services she touts can save lives, but every part of her job is difficult.

Mulki is an *asha*, part consultant, part scout, in the business of health reconnaissance. Easing the fear that comes with creating life isn't easy here, where education is rare, formal care is scarce and villages are remote. Every day, Mulki travels over foothills at the base of India's biggest mountain range, canvassing Kalthana's 14 hamlets that span several miles, approaching at least 10 doors each day. Leads about growing families come from local gossip. The task is physically demanding but also psychologically draining.

The women behind the doors often don't believe her; what she offers seems impossible. Every mother wants more for her children, but not every mother knows what more could mean. Not every mother knows what to hope for.

Mulki meets women like Kamla Gameti. Married at 16, Kamla was in her early twenties and pregnant with her second child when she first opened her door to Mulki. Kamla's three-year-old son, Naresh, played at their feet while Mulki tried to sell Kamla on formal prenatal care, as well as a hospital delivery for her second birth, patiently explaining potential complications of a traditional home delivery and the hospital's resources in case of emergency.

Ninety-nine percent of maternal deaths occur in developing countries, with over 90 percent of those in Africa and Asia. Most are preventable. Rajasthan, Kamla's home province, is one of the poorest in this newly industrialized nation, where child brides

Mulki Bhil: traveling health advocate

ABOVE: *Every day, Mulki Bhil sets out across the 14 hamlets of Kalthana village, offering health care services to new and expectant mothers.*

FACING PAGE: *Mulki visits a young child and grandmother on her rounds.*

and adolescent mothers are especially vulnerable during childbirth. Here, maternal and infant mortality rates are higher than national averages.

The option of a hospital birth in a nearby town is another perk of the anganwadi's services. To be eligible, new mothers must agree to checkups and consent to keeping medical records, an incentive meant to boost health, not just hospital births. It seemed like an offer would-be mothers wouldn't refuse, but they do.

Kalthana's anganwadi opened in 1997. Years earlier, a government scheme had designated the centers mandatory resources for the country's urban slums and rural villages. Though the state will erect a building to meet requirements—one for every 1,000 people—infrastructure and awareness of services are often lacking. Many young women in Kalthana have never attended school. New mothers couldn't read newspaper articles about child welfare policies. Attendance was low.

Over decades, Kalthana's anganwadi fell into disrepair. Its thatched mud roof leaked in the rain. Ink-and-paper medical records were vulnerable during monsoon season. Nutrient packets set to deliver vital protein and vitamins to pregnant women and

ABOVE: *Kalthana's anganwadi (a health center and daycare) opened in 1997 but over decades fell into disrepair. After WE Charity renovated the building, it became a refuge for new mothers and young children.*
FACING PAGE: *New mothers look to Mulki for health advice and to ease the fear that comes with creating life.*

Ninety-nine percent of maternal deaths occur in developing countries, and most are preventable.

toddlers—a dry mix of ground wheat, sugar, soy and lentils—spoiled in the damp. Nurses failed to turn up to treat would-be mothers. The long walk from home for a pregnant woman seeking services might result in nothing more than swollen ankles.

Mulki was left peddling false hope. "They used to be afraid," she said of the local women. "They were not confident in me."

Anganwadis are the centerpiece of WE Charity's health pillar in India. An existing government investment makes municipal partnerships and rehabilitation of anganwadis the best course of action. WE leverages that commitment to health programming and bolsters it. In Kalthana, the anganwadi's roof and floors were refurbished and supplies replenished—medicine was restocked, furniture was provided. With better resources, local nurses renewed their promises of regular appointments. WE Charity's own mobilizers now join Mulki on her rounds to spread the word. The same team runs health education for mothers and children. At the anganwadi, there are lessons on handwashing and the need to boil well water to prevent the spread of bacterial diseases and waterborne illnesses. Prenatal dietary needs are discussed to prevent malnutrition.

Kamla had never received formal medical care. Before Naresh was born, she had no prenatal consult, no blood test for hemoglobin levels or screening for pelvic cancer. There was no stethoscope to check for a fetal heartbeat. It was Kamla and her baby against the odds.

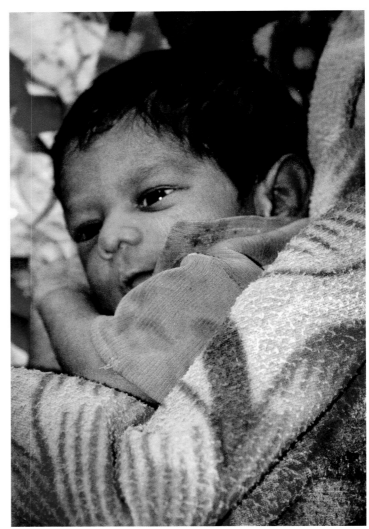

"*Darpani*" and "*santa ve*" are the Mewari words Kamla used to describe her first pregnancy. Fear, because she didn't know anything about the health of her baby. Worry, that stress from her fear would harm the life inside her. She and Mulki spoke through a translator, relaying the details of their first meeting.

Kamla faced a choice between two fears: the anxiety that would surround a pregnancy without formal care, and her stress about a hospital delivery in a cold, sterile room miles from home. The doctor would be a stranger. A village midwife known as a *dai* had delivered Naresh at Kamla's parents' home in Jardhol, a few towns over. Despite a lack of formal training, dais are trusted community members and comforting choices for anxious moms.

Many mothers in all parts of the world choose home births for similar reasons, but they can also make a game-day decision to head to a hospital in the case of a difficult labor. For Kamla and other women without access to health care, there's nowhere to turn for formal knowledge of healthy birth weights or organ development, infections, high blood pressure or breeching. A litany of risks are unheard of—anemia, asphyxiation, preeclampsia. Here, "normal" delivery means the baby survives. "Abnormal" means a stillbirth. There is only life and death. Variances between the extremes are unknown unless someone intervenes. Mulki walks so that young mothers like Kamla won't become statistics.

With Mulki's insistence and the fresh memory of panic from her first pregnancy, Kamla agreed to go to the anganwadi for prenatal care. Kamla's youngest baby, Vinod, was born at Sayra Hospital in the nearest city, Kelwara. After delivery, she and Vinod spent 48 hours under observation. Her family received health records, complete with inoculation dates for the boys.

At the anganwadi, Kamla's sons receive health care, daycare and preschool lessons. When they're older, they will graduate to the nearby Kalthana Primary School and its bright classrooms built by WE Charity.

And when Kamla has another child—she will one day, she says, and hopes for a girl—Mulki won't have to beg her to come. Since the refurbishment, anganwadi attendance is up, making Mulki's pitch much more appealing. Her job just got a little easier.

Mulki sets out again. Doors are waiting.

KATIE HEWITT

FACING PAGE, TOP: *Checking on a newborn*
FACING PAGE, BOTTOM: *Mulki is on the road again.*

Health training helps women avert illness and discover common ground

PILLAR: HEALTH

Women of different ages and castes gather on a weekday afternoon to examine their hands and nails. The discussion would have seemed frivolous a few years ago, but today in Kalthana village, as in all WE Charity partner communities in Rajasthan, such meetings are seen as vital to well-being for participants and, by extension, their families.

Welcome to the women's circle, equal parts training session and support group, where members learn how both to kill germs and manage their husbands. The first segment they study with WE Charity staff; the second part they learn from each other.

During monthly sessions, women explore how simple practices can defeat illnesses that once robbed them of so many days. Tricks like boiling water and scrubbing with soap can ward off parasites and bacteria, the chief culprits behind diarrheal diseases. Growing pulses in a home garden can bolster protein intake and alleviate malnutrition. And installing a stove that funnels smoke out of the house can reduce the incidence of respiratory and eye infections. WE Charity provides the training and materials for women to bring these changes home, and regular meetings allow for follow-up—an essential part of health education. Supplanting practices that have persisted for generations requires time, commitment and conversation.

In today's session, we find Bhanwari Bhil (the elder) and Bhanwari Bhil (the younger). A grandmother and a young mother respectively, they go by the same name but come from different castes. Previously, group members seldom visited one another, rarely (if ever) mingling with women on different rungs of the social hierarchy. But now, gathered under the banner of health education, they are seated on the same ground, sharing common struggles—how to feed their families and forestall tragedy, how to maintain household peace. They talk about their crops, their infants, their in-laws. Older women impart wisdom. Younger ones offer new ideas.

While improved health and hygiene practices have reduced hospital visits, the emerging empathy born of these meetings can only be measured by the closeness of the circle, the bursts of laughter, the depth of silence as each member shares her story.

DEEPA SHANKARAN

An auto-rickshaw brings a husband home

He once struggled to find work in his village, but when presented with a new opportunity, he became a lifeline for his family and his whole community.

For his first six weeks as an auto-rickshaw driver, Laxman Bhil rode alone. He didn't stop for the village schoolchildren or farmers hauling their produce to market, and nobody waved him down. Instead, people shouted at his hooded carriage as it rumbled past, warning him not to tumble off a cliff.

No one knew how a motorized three-wheeler would fare on the hilly terrain of Kalthana village. Until then, the only public transport was the government bus that lumbered into town once a day. For this rural community in the folds of the Aravalli Mountains, walking two hours to school or work was a rite of passage as much as a barrier to progress. Even the man behind the wheel couldn't believe his good fortune. Laxman had gone from farmer to driver overnight, and at first refused to risk any life but his own. He practiced relentlessly, propelled by terror, but also hope.

"It was like a dream," Laxman recalls. "When we used to go to Udaipur city, we would see auto-rickshaws and think how good it would be if they came to our village, how our lives would be easier."

When the community of Kalthana partnered with WE Charity in 2013, a widespread longing for change gave rise to projects on a number of fronts. New classrooms were built for the primary school where Laxman's grandchildren would soon be enrolled. The village health center where his wife worked was renovated, and an agricultural training program was launched to help farmers get more out of their fields. But the lack of public transportation kept Kalthana's residents from reaching their goals.

In 2015, a corporate donor provided WE Charity with auto-rickshaws for their partner communities in Rajasthan. The initiative's primary intent was income generation, supporting the organization's opportunity pillar programming. Community members who received rickshaws would charge a small fee per ride and gain a new source of income, but improved mobility would also energize the village economy. That first year, four auto-rickshaws were distributed. If the pilot project was successful, another four vehicles would be donated the following year.

PILLAR

 OPPORTUNITY

Laxman Bhil: rickshaw driver and community lifeline

Despite their struggles, or perhaps because of them, Laxman and his wife were a forward-thinking pair.

At the time, Laxman was a subsistence farmer; he and his wife, Daili, aimed to produce enough to feed their household. But their parched hillside plot often failed to sustain the family—three adult sons, three daughters-in-law and four grandchildren. Their two-room home could barely contain the growing numbers. "Our house was made of clay, straw and sticks," Laxman says. "It wasn't safe. Snakes and scorpions used to get in." Having left school in Grade 3, Laxman's only option for paid employment was manual labor. When there were no local construction jobs, he was forced to leave the village in search of work, and Daili had to manage both the farm and her job as a health worker for weeks or months at a time.

Despite their struggles, or perhaps because of them, Laxman and his wife were a forward-thinking pair. If you ask him why he was selected for the auto-rickshaw program, Laxman will likely cite their commitment to education. The eldest of their three adult sons graduated from secondary school, while the younger two completed Grade 8. And to advance her position at the health center, Daili was pursuing her high school diploma by correspondence, with her husband's full support. In a rural setting like Kalthana,

Laxman's daily rounds might include school drop-offs, trips to market or a race to the hospital. Until Kalthana village got a rickshaw of its own, residents had no choice but to walk all those distances.

Laxman was also a prime candidate because of his clear commitment to his fellow villagers, a fact that he humbly concedes when pressed: "When we are helping each other, we all live together in unity."

these were signs of a remarkable openness to new ideas. Laxman was also a prime candidate for the program because of his devotion to his community, a fact that he humbly concedes when pressed: "When we are helping each other, we all live together in unity."

From his first day behind the wheel, Laxman handled the rickshaw with reverence. He drove alone over every hill in Kalthana, testing both the vehicle and his own skill, and began to take on passengers only once he was sure he could deliver them intact.

Since that time, Laxman has helped the village tick with more urgency. When he finds students running late, he ushers them to school free of charge, a kind gesture that becomes an essential service during monsoon season. He gets traders to the market while their produce is still fresh and can fetch a better price. He brings health and daycare supplies, water pumps and piping, fertilizer and seeds into the community, and takes farmers to training workshops and back. While the rickshaw was introduced as a vehicle for opportunity, Laxman has helped take the impact to every other WE Charity development pillar: education, clean water, food security and health.

Laxman Ram with his wife, Daili, who works at the village health center

One evening, about six months into his new career, Laxman received a call from a woman who had gone into labor. He hopped into his rickshaw and went to collect her, along with her two female chaperones. They were no more than 10 minutes from the hospital when the women shouted for Laxman to stop. "We're nearly there, don't worry," he told them. He had learned to drive safely under pressure. The women insisted he stop and get out of the vehicle. He cut the motor and the road went silent. The rickshaw's headlight glow was the only light for miles. Laxman walked a few paces and looked out into the dark fields. Within a half-hour, the baby's first cry reached him where he stood.

Daili isn't a fan of this story. She would have preferred if the call had come earlier, in time for the delivery to happen properly at the hospital. But she shares her husband's sense of duty and thus welcomes all requests, even when they come in the dead of night. "If you do good, good things come to you," she says.

In his time as a driver, Laxman has ferried more than 15 women per year to the hospital to deliver their babies. He once saved a man's life by scooping him up after a motorcycle accident. He supplied his phone number to the local government and to all the households in the area, making his rickshaw as much a community shuttle as a lifeline. "I don't leave the village," he says. "In case there's an emergency, I should be here."

In return, Laxman's homestead has blossomed. His wife, children and grandchildren moved out of their two-room mud house into a sturdy concrete structure with seven rooms, enough for an extended family to grow. "With the earnings from the rickshaw, we built a *pucca* house," he says, meaning "solid" or, more literally, "ripe." Even when business is slow, Laxman never leaves Kalthana in search of other work. At the end of every shift, whenever it ends, Daili knows he'll be coming home.

DEEPA SHANKARAN

Secrets in the soil

In a desert state beset by drought, subtle changes to traditional techniques and tools are helping farmers move from mere subsistence to food security.

On any given morning, Noja Bhil is accompanied into his verdant field by up to five fellow farmers from the village of Bhilo Ki Barind. In recent years, this soft-spoken soul has become a fount of useful information: when to plant, how often to irrigate, what blade is best to flip the arid Mewari soil. The neighbors are keen to learn his secrets, having seen the height of his wheat stalks, the new beans in his children's bowls. Noja is eager to oblige.

PILLAR

♦ **FOOD**

He didn't always move with this level of self-assurance. His family, like other households in this community, once lived at the mercy of shifting weather patterns that brought drought and hunger to their doorstep. The diet of plain roti his children grew up on offered them little energy to thrive. A subsistence farmer relying on the yield from his own land, Noja finally had to move beyond the methods he learned from his father. The updates are subtle but significant.

Noja is one of 200 farmers across this rural stretch of Rajasthan to take part in WE Charity's food programming. Food security is a core pillar in the organization's sustainable development model, which includes education, water, health and opportunity. Launched in India in 2013, the food pillar works to improve the quantity and nutritional value of meals consumed in the organization's partner communities, bolstering the efforts of families to create long-term change.

For the farmers of Bhilo Ki Barind, WE Charity organized training sessions led by expert agronomists to introduce modern but regionally appropriate tools and techniques. The work ethic of the trainees was beyond reproach, but what they learned is that timing is everything. "Before, we used to irrigate the field whenever we wanted," says Noja. "We learned when to sow, when to harvest, how to take care of the crops."

Farmers were also provided with improved seeds for wheat and corn, staples they had grown for generations. While the new seeds required less water—a boon in this desert state—they also produced double the harvest, as compared to the seeds that were used before.

Noja Bhil: subsistence farmer and father of five

ABOVE: *Noja and neighboring farmers in the community of Bhilo Ki Barind*

RIGHT: *Noja shows a fellow farmer the healthy gourd he grew using WE Charity agricultural training and tools.*

FACING PAGE TOP: *The seed drill allows farmers to plant seeds at equal distances and at the proper depth, ensuring adequate exposure to light, nutrients and water. Before its introduction, farmers had to estimate spacing when planting, which resulted in low productivity.*

FACING PAGE BOTTOM: *The new plow provided by WE Charity has a curved blade that flips and aerates the soil, making it more fertile and killing insects or weeds that damage crops.*

Noja's farm now produces a variety of beans and lentils, a new source of protein for his family.
FIRST ROW: **L.** *Cow peas,* **R.** *Soya beans;* **SECOND ROW:** **L.** *Corn,* **R.** *Okra;* **THIRD ROW:** **L.** *Black gram,* **R.** *Soya beans*

Continued collaboration between WE Charity, agronomists and community members has transformed the landscape of Bhilo Ki Barind, but an untrained eye might miss the subtleties. The village oxen plow the fields as they have for centuries, but alongside the traditional flat wooden tool, a curved metal blade brings fresh nutrients to the surface, leaving the earth more fertile. And while Noja's children still find roti at most meals, their mother, Rajaki, crushes soya beans into the flour. "She is really happy," Noja says. "It tastes much better than the normal roti. Everyone in the family likes soya beans."

While Rajaki learned new recipes from the WE Charity team, the ingredients were supplied by her husband, whose harvest has not only doubled but also diversified. In the plot next to their home now grows a vegetable garden, sprouting protein-rich beans and lentils. Farmers across Bhilo Ki Barind have followed suit, fueling their households with a new and wholesome energy. "Earlier, we weren't producing enough to sustain the family, but now it's sufficient," says Noja, humbly noting that being able to provide quality food for his family is a source of great joy.

For him, a full day in the field is a good day. And when his neighbors seek him out for guidance, he is proud to share. "In the past, I was learning from them. Now they are able to learn from me. We've been sharing our knowledge for a long time." In this village in Rajasthan, modern inputs are quietly revitalizing traditional mechanisms, producing new shoots in the soil that was always there.

DEEPA SHANKARAN

Continued collaboration between WE Charity, agronomists and community members has transformed the landscape of Bhilo Ki Barind. Noja's harvest has not only doubled but also diversified.

LEFT: *Noja and his wife, Rajaki*
ABOVE: *Rajaki incorporates beans and lentils from Noja's harvest into family meals. The added nutrition has improved their children's health and ability to focus in school.*

A pact and a challenge

When WE Charity and the community of Kalinjar teamed up to build a school, one partner agreed to bring the bricks, the other to bring the students.

The monsoon comes as a blessing for farmers in the desert state of Rajasthan, but for the young minds of Kalinjar village, it's more of a curse.

During the wet season, the community's school is nearly empty. Rain batters the roof and seeps through the cracked ceiling, pooling in corners and sending rivulets over the floor. The few students in class stretch sheets of plastic over their heads to keep their books from ruin, but in this storm of distractions, it's hard to focus. Built in 1962, Kalinjar's school is like so many rural facilities across the state. Dark, musty, poorly ventilated rooms hold little appeal for students, who study hunched on the floor for lack of benches. When the rains pass, classrooms go from empty to overcrowded, with multiple grades forced to share a single room. In this condition, the school seems less a gateway to opportunity than a barrier.

Ogu Bhil, 65, is a father to six sons and three daughters, and while he has attempted to educate all of them, it's been hit and miss. His older children dropped out in the early stages of primary school, following in their father's footsteps. His sons Kesu, Heera and Ganesh are in Grades 7, 6 and 5, respectively, and of late, Ogu has been enforcing attendance with unprecedented rigor. He would like to see them graduate, and for the first time in the history of his family, this is a real possibility.

In 2018, Kalinjar partnered with WE Charity on a series of projects to target the root causes of poverty and loosen its hold on the community. As in many other villages in Rajasthan, roughly 65 percent of Kalinjar's residents cannot read or write. Most are subsistence farmers with small plots of land, just hoping to grow enough to feed their families. They live at the mercy of unpredictable rains, which compel many farmers, Ogu included, to seek additional work as unskilled laborers. WE Charity works with communities in the region to improve access to five key resources—education, clean water, health care, food and opportunity—setting them on the path to sustainable development.

PILLAR

★ **EDUCATION**

Ogu and his youngest sons, Heera (left) and Ganesh

ABOVE: *Heera (right) and Ganesh bring water home from the village hand pump.*
RIGHT: *Ogu's son Uma (left) studied until Grade 5 at Kalinjar's school, and now he works as a farmer and laborer alongside his father.*
FACING PAGE, TOP LEFT: *Ogu (right) and his brother Varda.*
FACING PAGE, TOP RIGHT: *Heera (right) and Ganesh make time for homework after the school day.*
FACING PAGE, BOTTOM: *Ogu (right) stands with his sons Heera (right), Uma (center) and Ganesh (left) and his daughter-in-law Premi.*

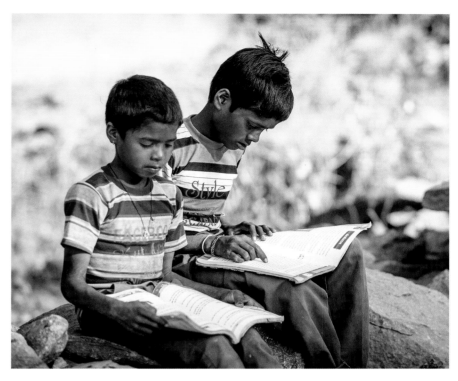

Ogu can see the new school going up from his rooftop terrace, but he and his sons still visit the construction site every day to monitor progress and encourage the workers.

For families struggling to maintain even a basic standard of living, this proposal might seem like a heady dream. For this reason, WE Charity often begins partnerships with a school-building project. Once completed, a school stands as tangible proof of the organization's commitment and creates momentum for the work ahead. Before a single brick is laid, however, a community must commit to filling every classroom with students. It's a pact, but also a challenge, because it requires a shift in mindset about the value of education.

"When I was young, no one told us about the importance of education. People were focused on their fields," Ogu says. He dropped out in Grade 2 to work on his father's farm, the same land he cultivates today. "These days, you have to be clever," he explains, citing market vendors who take advantage of illiteracy. "They tell you that you're not educated so you don't understand money. Someone who is educated will know how much money to give and how much to take back."

His older children never learned these lessons and may face the same challenges as their father. But Ogu has reason to believe in a different future for his youngest three—one in which they are equipped to navigate a changing world. From the crumbling stone terrace of his house, he

can see the opportunity going up. The construction site is a draw for the village children, and Ogu often spots Heera and Ganesh there, watching their new school take shape.

"It should be big enough for every class to have its own room, and sturdy enough to withstand the monsoon," Ogu says. He shares the hope of parents across WE Charity's partner communities, that their children will be comfortable in their new classrooms and able to focus year-round. Every day on his way back from the fields, Ogu stops to check in on the workers. He tells them to build it quickly—but build it well. And every day, they assure him they are on the job.

"Sometimes I will miss a day and go after two days, and then I'll see the progress," Ogu says. "The bricks are laid. A wall is completed. It makes me feel happy."

DEEPA SHANKARAN

Ogu is more motivated than ever to work hard to support his children's future.

Infrastructure in India

Beneath the inspirational stories of transformation in Rajasthan, India, that this book celebrates are the bricks and mortar that form the foundations upon which so much of WE Charity's work is built: from lavatories to primary schoolrooms to high schools to maternal and child health clinics to household gardens and wells.

WE Charity supporters not only fund transformative programs that help families to create their own solutions to end poverty, they also come together to finance the construction of significant infrastructure projects.

Students wash their hands at the school's hand pump.

Students wave from the porch of their new classroom at Udawad Primary School.

Increasing plot yields is at the heart of WE Charity's food program in Rajasthan.

A teacher helps a student in a new classroom.

Gates open to the renovated high school campus in Verdara.

Washrooms at Verdara High School

Classrooms are outfitted with desks and chairs, a first for many local primary schools.

The rehabilitated health center in Lai provides health services to mothers and children under five.

Deepening old wells ensures a greater flow of water for families and their fields.

KENYA

A woman empowered is the strongest force for change

"I have watched mamas in rural Kenya become financially integral to their households, supporting their families, sending their children to school, and becoming leaders and makers of their own futures."

BY ROXANNE JOYAL, CO-FOUNDER AND CEO OF ME TO WE

Our deep connection to Kenya formed long before Marc and I were married, back when we were still students. Truth be told, we've been following each other around the world since we started dating in university, acting as mutual moral supports in our early work overseas. We first came to the country as volunteers for a gap year after our freshman year at college. Marc worked as an environmental officer on a wildlife reserve. I worked with local women to help establish a co-op gift shop so that small-scale entrepreneurs, mostly young mothers, could sell their crafts and jewelry at a fair price. Investing in women—as entrepreneurs, as community leaders and as trailblazers—would become the focus of my career and, eventually, a centerpiece project for WE.

Gap year over, I went on to study international development at Stanford University, read law at the University of Oxford, and later clerked for the Supreme Court of Canada. But my calling was not that of a traditional career path—I devoted my time to WE. Along with Marc and Craig, I returned many times to Kenya to establish schools in the Maasai Mara, a sprawling game reserve and national park that also piqued the interest of other parties—with different motives. Negotiations were considerable at first.

Early on, we faced strong opposition from local tourism companies whose motivation was to maintain the status quo. They thought—and rightly so—that WE's development work would raise wages, education levels and expectations. For those business owners, the area's Indigenous people were a cheap source of labor and a profitable tourist attraction, all the more easily exploited for being marginalized. With their bright red robes, beaded jewelry and elongated earlobes, the region's Maasai people are among the most recognizable tribes in all of Africa. They are also among the continent's poorest. Their rural communities remain challenged by malaria, tuberculosis, drought and encroaching development that makes it more and more difficult to maintain pastureland for their cattle. When we started working in the area, the average daily wage was US$1.25.

But there were others behind us from the beginning—our community partners. In Kenya, every project began with a candid meeting between WE's team, village elders and, perhaps most important, local women leaders—the heart and backbone of any community. I remember distinctly one August morning in 2002, when Marc and I approached Ol Musereji, a small settlement of huts and a derelict school in Narok County near the Maasai Mara National Reserve. It was the start of a potential partnership, and one of our first meetings.

We'd expected to meet with a few dozen leaders. Instead, 300 women turned up, all eager to share opinions and ideas. We took shelter from the sun under a stand of haggard acacia trees and sat for hours as Maasai was translated into English, and English back into Maasai. The women shared their many challenges: caring for children, cattle and crops, in the absence of their husbands.

According to Maasai custom, once men become warriors, they don't have many responsibilities inside the home. This is a holdover from earlier times, back when the men would patrol during tribal wars and hunt game for food, but those ways of life are changing. Thankfully, there's more peace in the region and much less need for constant protection. Meanwhile, traditional duties for women became more taxing as settlements moved farther from water sources and populations expanded, both of which shrunk the already small farming plots and pressured families to send children to work. The women were carrying much of the weight as cultural norms evolved. Still, they were very disbelieving of our offer to build a school for their kids. An elder told us that many non-profits had promised them assistance, but the offers never amounted to much. To this day, I'm not sure why they committed to us—I suppose it was our patience that won them over. The sun was setting by the time our conversation came to a close. I felt a huge responsibility not to disappoint them, because when we left, we were certain they thought they would never see us again.

A young relationship had been established with this group, and

Students from the primary school in Emori Joi, one of the first schools and communities to partner with WE Charity in Kenya, now have access to quality education.

further support was formalized in surrounding villages. We met with the highest-ranking regional chief, who mobilized the community to choose a piece of land on which the school would be located and held in community trust. And so began the first pillar of our development model: education. The timing turned out to be crucial. In 2003, Kenya's newly elected government had made primary education mandatory and free for all. As a result, millions of additional children suddenly appeared at schools across the country. Classes were congested, with children squeezed into mud huts or else scattered in an open field. Teachers were caught off guard when multiple grades turned up in a single classroom, one without proper ventilation, furniture or materials. The sudden announcement had left no time for preparation. WE Charity supported the new primary education initiative with construction of schoolrooms in the region, while the government pledged to maintain infrastructure, hiring teachers and providing materials and resources.

Our core belief in partnerships has always extended beyond community members, who are collaborators in all projects, not recipients of aid. Local governments at every level must also be engaged. It's critical to pool resources with already established infrastructure, for the sake of both viability and sustainability. WE Charity could never pull off everything on its own, nor would we want to. In Kenya, and in every country in which we operate, WE Charity works with government-assigned teachers and nurses, as well as affiliated

engineering companies, architects, drivers and other workers who keep our projects running, with buy-in from everyone involved.

This spurs job creation, but also ownership and independent oversight. Since the long-term plan is to leave the projects and the legacy with the community once WE Charity departs, early support from local leaders and governments who can maintain those projects is essential.

With Kenya's education pillar established, the other pillars of our development model followed: water, health, opportunity and food security. This five-pillar model has empowered communities to become self-sustaining after five to eight year as we continue to partner with new communities, always working to lift people higher.

Just as we were devoted to education internationally, we also wanted to accommodate students, teachers and families from our home country who wanted to volunteer alongside our Kenyan partners, so they could connect and learn from one another. In the years that followed, we built Bogani, which would become an education center, a tented camp for visiting students, and eventually accommodation for adults and families eager to learn about development work and cultural immersion, to better understand the opportunities and challenges of life in rural Kenya.

A bead for your thoughts

After Marc and I were married in 2007, we invited our families along on our honeymoon—not a common practice for newlyweds, I know. We wanted them to see our projects and meet the people who'd become our extended family over in Kenya. As we sat around a bonfire one evening, we heard a gentle rustling coming from a thicket behind us. We jumped up, afraid that a predator had wandered too close to our camp. Instead, we saw a large group of Maasai warriors, mamas and elders push through the underbrush. The chief explained that we had spent so much time in the community that we were now part of the Maasai family—and so needed to be married according to local custom. Marc and I were placed back-to-back as the Maasai danced and sang around us; they placed grass in our shoes to symbolize that we were part of the Earth, and the elders spat fermented goat's milk on our feet—a sign of respect. Finally, I was gifted a stunning collection of beaded wedding collars, with tiny glass beads threaded into perfect geometric designs in bright colors. In the Maasai culture, a man's wealth is measured in cattle and children, while a woman wears her wealth and experience around her neck. All of the important events in a woman's life are marked with necklaces: marriage, childbirth, grandchildren. A Maasai mama's life is written in beads.

Looking back, it's difficult to put this moment into words, to explain how much it meant to me or how significant those tiny beads would become to the whole trajectory of WE Charity, or how many women's lives they would change. Since my first trip to Kenya, I had marveled at the artistry of the mamas and had long aspired to help them find a broader market for their work. After our Maasai wedding, with my own treasured collection of beads, I revisited that plan. Economic empowerment, or opportunity, would become crucial to the sustainability of our entire model. Though it wasn't our first pillar, some would call opportunity the most foundational, since alternative income programs and business training serve to sustain every other project.

I approached several women for advice and support. Leah Lato Toyianka was the first on board. Well-respected in her village and familiar with WE Charity, Mama Leah was the first to make the momentous choice to work outside the home. She had to consider how her husband would feel about her breaking tradition. She wondered what her friends would think, and whether she would have enough time for her children. On the other hand, if she partnered with us to take Maasai designs further, her local custom and pastime could become a means of supporting her family. She later told me that, while making her decision, she lay awake at night, imagining her beads traveling around the world.

Mama Leah helped rally the first 250 artisans, who laid the foundation for designs, marketing, pricing and wages. At the time, women were vastly underpaid and there was no comparable living wage in Kenya. So they worked backwards: how much would they need to earn to feed their families? Send their children to school? Set aside savings? The women needed to land on a price that would

WE Charity provides financial literacy training and alternative income programming as well as support for community-led merry-go-round groups that offer small loans to women entrepreneurs.

meet those requirements. There were hundreds of voices to consider and no rule book to consult.

At first, ME to WE Artisans functioned on trial and error and the perseverance of a handful of women leaders. We didn't know whether we could establish consistent quality, meet production deadlines or modify Maasai designs for Western consumers. But with time, ME to WE Artisans tapped into a ready market of fashionable, socially conscious women in North America who embraced the Kenyan mamas, their story and their craft. Mothers on one side of the world wanted to connect with mothers across oceans, women supporting women to lift their families and communities out of poverty. The impact grew. In 2020, more than 1,600 women in WE Charity partner communities are gainfully employed by ME to WE Artisans. With the financial literacy training we offer, they have been able to quadruple their incomes, electing chairs and treasurers for every beading group and emerging as leaders in their own right. Their earnings are more than enough to meet their goals, and even to reach dreams they hadn't considered—to send children to college or to start a second business in animal husbandry. The courage and commitment of these women have jump-started a new micro-economy.

In Kenya, traditional handicrafts laid the foundation for a revolutionary social enterprise model that has not only reshaped our approach to development but also disrupted cultural norms and women's roles. ME to WE's artisans, primarily women who hadn't previously worked outside the home, now regularly out-earn their husbands. These wives were once ignored by their spouses and considered a burden. I've since heard of husbands opening the door as

ABOVE: *ME to WE artisan Naitalala Nabala shows off her beadwork. WE Charity's sister organization, the social enterprise ME to WE, was started to help women like Naitalala gain access to a wider market for their traditional jewelry and earn sustainable income.*
FACING PAGE: *A student at the Kisaruni all-girls secondary school stands in front of a wall depicting the school's motto in Maa and Kipsigis, local dialects, as well as English. It reads: "The only limits in our life are those we impose on ourselves."*

their artisan wives come home from work, ready and waiting to greet them. Gender norms in their communities are changing. Children, boys and girls alike, watch these evolving interactions—the impact is intergenerational. It is a well-known fact in international relations that a dollar earned by a woman is a dollar that goes straight to her household, her children and her community. I have watched the artisan mamas become financially integral to their households as they support their families and send their children to school. They become leaders in their communities and makers of their own futures, and I am continuously inspired by their strength and resilience. And with ME to WE sales supporting WE Charity projects, these women are also working to uplift whole communities.

This chapter is dedicated to the mamas who have guided and inspired us, and to all the community members who have transformed their lives and livelihoods in partnership with WE. Women like Judy Cheborkei, whose story you will find in the following pages. Part of the Kipsigis tribe, a group historically in conflict with their neighboring Maasai, Mama Judy was taught to bead by Maasai artisans. Shared goals to increase incomes and better their children's futures have brokered a new peace between the groups. They come together at the new Women's Empowerment Centre, our beading headquarters in the middle of the Mara, where veteran artisans teach others who are interested. When we opened, hundreds of women turned

up who'd never threaded a single bead. Soon we were sending them our most intricate designs for troubleshooting.

In this chapter, you will also learn about the genesis of our first Kenyan health clinic, now known as Baraka Hospital, the only center that offers quality maternal and infant care in the region. With patients traveling in from other communities, the area soon needed a second facility, which we named Kishon Clinic, while we turned Baraka into a registered center for professional development. Our long-term vision is for Baraka to become a full teaching and referral hospital that will build up the next generation of caregivers, where the children of artisan trailblazers can become nurses or clinicians without the cost of traveling to the city for schooling.

We also share successes from the boys and girls walking a new path in the midst of cultural reckonings. You will read about Francis Naimodu, who dreams of becoming an engineer after he graduates from WE Charity's all-boys campus, part of the Kisaruni Group of Schools (KGS), and wrestles with new notions of manhood. You will meet the girls who started as students in our primary schools and went on to graduate from the all-girls campus of KGS, an award-winning institution with competitive admissions for the region's brightest young women. Many of their mothers never went to school but are now employed as ME to WE artisans or are operating small businesses with support from WE Charity's financial literacy groups, which has enabled them to send their daughters to school. It's what every mother wants for her children—more opportunities than she had herself.

In perhaps the most remarkable story of all, you will meet the students of WE College. Many of these students started their primary education within the four walls of a WE Charity school, learned from the teachers who participated in our professional development training programs, grew up eating the midday lunches provided, carried clean water back home from the school water dispensaries, studied agriculture in the school gardens to learn how their families could increase their crop yields, and sought medical care from the mobile medical units (and now clinics and a hospital) in the region.

Over the years, those students thrived, reached the improbable milestone of attending Kisaruni High School, and today are pursuing their dreams of a college education. WE College students are currently studying in the School of Nursing (Faculty of Public Health) and the School of Tourism and Hospitality (Faculty of Technical Studies), and future high school graduates will soon have even more varied opportunities with the launch of the Faculties of Civil Engineering, Business and Information Technology, Medicine, and Education. Designed to meet local gaps in employment, the course offerings will prepare graduates for future careers as engineers, teachers, mechanics, health care practitioners, guides and hospitality managers. These graduates will write the next chapter of this region's incredible story of transformation.

The success of these students, and of all of our partners, marks a significant change in just one generation. It reminds me of a Maasai saying: "If you step somewhere where no one has stepped before, you will create your own mark." I am honored to walk alongside the mamas and all our community partners in Kenya, as their colleague, champion and friend. Empowered women empower women, and a woman empowered is the strongest force for change.

Impact at a glance

Focus on Narok County

Population: 850,920
Languages: English and Swahili are the two official languages, although 42 ethnic groups have their own dialects. Maa and Kipsigis are the two most commonly spoken dialects where WE Charity works in Kenya.
Population with secondary education: 7.2%
Literacy rate (15 and above): 41%, compared to national average of 79%
Children under five affected by stunting: 33%
Households with access to improved water infrastructure: 33.6%

*The above statistics are drawn from the World Bank and local government sources.

Narok County is a semi-arid region in southwestern Kenya that includes the famed Maasai Mara—host to the great wildebeest migration and Africa's "big five," the African elephant, Cape buffalo, African leopard, African lion and African black rhino. This region is also home to the Maasai and Kipsigis peoples. These ethnic groups have rich cultures, but they have also experienced historical marginalization and exploitation. Traditional ways of life are changing. Men no longer hunt big game for food, while pastureland for their cows, sheep and goats is being destroyed by development and drought. Relative isolation has inhibited access to education. Lack of clean water, drought, high maternal and infant mortality rates, and limited opportunities trap many families in a cycle of poverty.

WE Charity partners with dozens of rural communities in Narok County to implement a five-pillar model for sustainable development. This programming has expanded into neighboring Bomet County, which faces similar challenges. Through this collaboration, communities drive long-term solutions to complex issues, creating opportunities for younger generations.

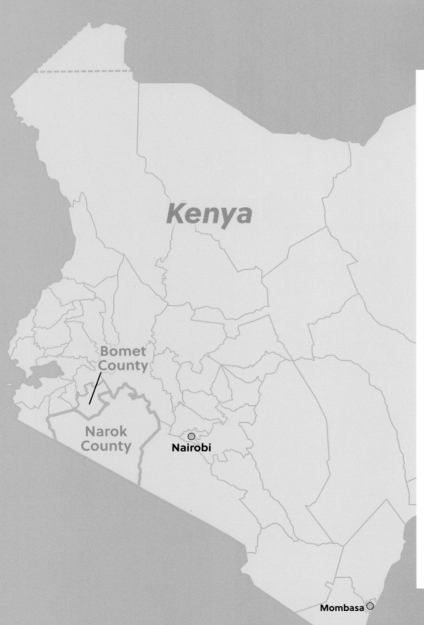

Impact by the numbers by 2020

★ EDUCATION

13,000+ students supported from elementary school through to high school. WE College opened in 2017 to help students pursue professional designations and become career-ready.

◉ WATER

16 boreholes—half are solar-powered—providing clean water to students and families in 15 communities

♥ HEALTH

144,000+ patient visits to Baraka Hospital and Kishon Health Centre

10,000+ patients served by 260+ mobile clinics serving 34 remote communities

◉ FOOD

19,000+ kilograms of produce harvested from 3 community farms, where farmers gain skills to apply to their family plots

♀ OPPORTUNITY

125+ savings groups for women, men and youth established to boost family incomes

1,600+ women working with ME to WE Artisans

Mercy and the miracle underground

When WE Charity and the people of Kipsongol teamed up to drill the first borehole in village history, they unearthed much more than clean water.

When the machines arrived in the village of Kipsongol, Mercy Rop rushed her young daughter to the site. She held her up to see the towering drill plunge into the earth, drawing up layers of silt in shades of pink, white and black—so different from the red Kenyan dirt that covered their shoes. As engineers fed long pipes into the ground, Mercy jostled amidst the crowd flooding the field to see the community's first borehole. She wanted little Truphena to witness the revolution.

"No one had a clue what was going on," says Mercy. "We were used to water flowing through the rivers, so we were eager to see what could come from underground." A mother of three, she understood the value of water, and what girls and women sacrifice for every drop. If they were freed from their long walk to collect water each day, they could work toward their futures instead.

Mercy inherited the task of fetching water as a child, as soon as her small arms could carry the jug. She would walk the rocky path to the river, edge down the bank past donkeys and around clusters of women washing clothes, and fill a five-gallon can for her family. The first of several daily trips would start at dawn.

As a teenager, Mercy dreamed of becoming a teacher. She wanted to help the children of her community grow in ways their parents hadn't imagined. But she struggled to focus on her studies.

"There was no time for reading. My family needed water," she says. "For girls, it was all about fetching water."

Mercy trained herself to balance the load and marched toward her goal, finally graduating from Grade 12. She had planned on a degree in early childhood education but had no way to pay for studies. A high school diploma, however, was a novel achievement among her peers, and she managed to secure a part-time teaching position at a local school.

PILLARS

💧 WATER

⭐ EDUCATION

Mercy Rop: clean-water convert, crusader

The women and girls of Kipsongol came to this murky pond to wash clothes and collect water for cleaning, cooking and drinking. Mercy used to make several trips a day, each time filling a five-gallon jerry can to haul home. Every drop carried the risk of disease, but she had no alternative until WE Charity drilled a borehole in her community.

In time, Mercy married a fellow teacher, moved to a new village and established her own household. Everything about that life was new, yet she soon found herself on a familiar path. The task of collecting river water was as demanding as ever, the haul just as murky, prompting frequent trips to the hospital to treat her growing family for typhoid and diarrhea. Mercy gave up teaching to look after her children's needs. When Truphena was born, she resolved to continue the walk for water herself, rather than pass down the duty to her only daughter. She wanted to see where Truphena's education could lead.

At a Kipsongol community meeting in the summer of 2015, Mercy heard the news she hadn't realized she'd been waiting for. WE Charity, which had been working in the area for several years and had renovated the local primary school, was hoping to boost attendance with a new project—a borehole. The initiative would include a large water tank, a community water kiosk and a handwashing station, all powered by solar electricity. If the school could become a source of clean water for the village, girls could carry home water after class, which would help convince their parents to enroll them. In addition, new washrooms would give them the privacy they needed as they matured. Knowing that even a brand-new school would sit empty if children didn't have the freedom or energy to attend, WE Charity introduced a five-pillar approach to the community that included education, health care, food security, economic opportunity and access to clean water.

"It was like a miracle," Mercy recalls. "Since I was a child, it was my dream to have clean water close to home."

For five days following the groundbreaking for the borehole, Mercy brought Truphena to watch the drills go deeper into the soil, and they shrieked together when a stream of water burst up from the ground. "The water was clean!" she says. "It wasn't salty like the river water. It was the first time in my life that I tasted water like that."

Her young daughter might have puzzled over the foreign machinery, but for Mercy, the significance of the moment was profound. "It meant the burden of fetching water was off our shoulders." She carried Truphena home that day, imagining a different future for her, one where she could have the time to study without having to struggle as women before her had done.

Since the arrival of clean water, markers of change have sprouted throughout the village. The water tower serves as a landmark at Kipsongol Primary School, calling children to school. Students stop at the handwashing station before meals, a new ritual to ward off illness. Parents visit the campus to fill their jerry cans at a cost of a few Kenyan shillings, building a steady fund for maintenance and repair. And the once barren lot beside the school now hosts a thriving community farm, where fresh vegetables and corn drink from the borehole.

Mercy brought Truphena to watch the drills go deeper into the soil, and they shrieked together when a stream of water burst up from the ground.

Mercy too has been unearthing a potential she never knew she had. With a clean water source just down the path from her home, she's won back hours of her day and can focus on productive activities that earn an income for her family. Her farm is blossoming, her cows are growing strong and her children are healthy. She has even revived her teaching skills, reviewing her children's homework in the evenings and helping them to earn top grades, confident their journey won't be defined by the search for water. This promise was within her all along, quietly waiting for a moment to be tapped.

DEEPA SHANKARAN

FACING PAGE: *The new borehole on the Kipsongol Primary School grounds is powered by solar electricity. Not only does the borehole provide clean drinking water for students and the entire village, it also irrigates the adjacent community farm, which was once barren.*

ABOVE: *Mercy stands with her son Japheth and her daughter, Truphena. Both are enrolled at Kipsongol Primary School.*

MIDDLE LEFT: *Mercy hands her money to Jonathan Rutto, the Kipsongol water kiosk vendor. She pays KSh2.5 (US$0.02) for 2.5 gallons of clean water, a small fee that funds project maintenance, ensures community ownership and safeguards long-term sustainability.*

BOTTOM LEFT: *Kipsongol Primary students drink and wash up at the hand pump, practicing basic hygiene that helps to keep them healthy and in school.*

The power of primary school

Education is at the heart of WE Charity's sustainable development model. While low literacy levels keep families in poverty, the organization believes that increasing access to quality education has the power to transform communities. But how to create access when schools are substandard and teachers are few?

In January of 2003, a Kenyan government mandate made primary education compulsory and free. An estimated one million new students flocked to derelict public schools across the country. In many rural schools, holes punctuated the walls and roofs leaked. Some classrooms were no more than sticks in the earth covered by metal sheets, built by parents with limited supplies. But students crowded in, eager to learn, with six bodies squished into a desk made for two and multiple grades jammed into one room. With all the distractions, little learning took place.

Building schoolrooms may be the most well-known of WE Charity's interventions. The organization upgrades existing school infrastructure or builds entirely new schoolrooms to create quality learning environments for students and teachers. But each build is successful only because it is founded on community partnership and government support.

At the start of every primary school project, the community organizes a groundbreaking ceremony. Parents flock to the school grounds and hoist their pickaxes. Mounds of dirt mark the growing magnitude of what is taking place— moms and dads creating educational opportunities for their children that they didn't experience themselves.

The schools are integrated into Kenya's public primary education system, providing a sustainable solution to overcrowded and under-resourced schools. WE Charity constructs the schoolrooms while the government is responsible for the operating costs, providing funding for teachers and overseeing the curriculum.

The concrete schoolrooms have big windows that allow the sunlight to shine in and are outfitted with desks and chalkboards. As WE Charity built or refurbished buildings, more students enrolled, though they were often boys. Girls remained tasked with household chores, like cooking, cleaning, caring for younger siblings and fetching water, which kept them from school.

To attract more girls to class and improve the health of families, WE Charity implemented its water pillar, drilling boreholes and creating clean-water stations at schools. Girls who once walked hours to collect river water in the middle of the school day could now carry clean water home from class.

As of 2020, WE Charity has built more than 200 primary schoolrooms in 29 communities in Narok County, in addition to administrative offices and teacher accommodations. WE Charity also runs teacher training and a competitive school spirit program and provides resources for school nutrition. And they're not just one building; primary schools are thriving campuses with classrooms, libraries, kitchens, latrines and clean water.

But the success and sustainability of a school are truly tested once WE Charity has exited a community. They are proven by consistency of student attendance, competitive academic performance and the increase in Grade 8 graduates. Even after WE Charity departs, the community keeps moving forward on all key metrics.

The immeasurable transformation happens outside the classroom, when children who picked up their pencils to learn to write and wrestled through math equations bring those lessons of literacy home to their parents.

The remains of an old school building stand in stark contrast to a new schoolroom built by WE Charity.

TOP: *Primary schools that partner with WE Charity participate in a School Pride Program, which rewards academic performance and campus beautification, as well as recognizing outstanding teachers.*

ABOVE: *When clean water is accessible at school, student attendance rates increase, particularly for girls.*

As of 2020, WE Charity had built over 200 classrooms across 29 communities in Kenya, helping more than 13,000 students attend primary school.

Who runs the world? Girls.

For many girls, attending the Kisaruni Group of Schools makes the difference between early marriage and a high school diploma. This is where students become the leaders of today.

Each girl who receives a full scholarship to attend high school at the Kisaruni Group of Schools (KGS) arrives with a story of fierce determination.

One 14-year-old ran away from home to escape circumcision, determined to foil her parents' plan for marriage. After taking her Grade 8 national exams, she disappeared into the bush for two months, wading across rivers and surviving on fruits and plants. Eventually she made her way to a town where a stranger gave her 500 Kenyan shillings (KSh), about US$5, to replace her shredded garments with new clothes. But the resolute teenager used the money to log on to a computer in an internet café to check her exam scores. She shouted for joy when she saw her marks, then quickly quieted. She had no money and no support. Still, she was going to go to high school, somehow, somewhere.

Another teenage girl, from another community, stopped and started primary school multiple times. Not because her parents didn't want her to get an education—they simply couldn't cover the costs for her and her five siblings. Whenever she was sent home from school, her mother would tutor her daughter in the evenings, hoping she could still pass the Grade 8 national exams. But when the primary school administration threw a party for her and the other successful students, the celebrations were short-lived. Her family couldn't afford to put her through high school.

Still another girl, the youngest of 14 siblings, dreamed of graduating from high school even though she'd watched as her elder sisters were pulled from Grade 6 to marry, in exchange for a dowry down payment that would support her family. Her older brothers, meanwhile, were allowed to complete primary school. She pressed her father to send her to the local primary school built by WE Charity. He agreed, as long as she did both housework and homework. She excelled at both and passed the Grade 8 national exams. Her father said she could attend high school, if she found the funds.

KGS consists of an all-girls campus and an all-boys campus on the outskirts of the Maasai Mara game reserve, tucked into the Ngulot Hills. The privately funded all-girls

campus is a boarding school that was opened by WE Charity in 2011 to help teenage girls access a high school education. The boys' campus opened in 2017.

From their celebration of local culture to their teaching style to the quality of resources, both the boys' and girls' campuses of KGS are the first of their kind in this region. Many families feared sending their children to boarding school, afraid they would lose their traditions and respect for community. KGS is designed to honor Maasai and Kipsigis cultures, showing that tradition and education are not at odds with each other.

Each week a community elder shares cultural traditions and values at a school-wide assembly. This promotes connection to one's own identity while also enhancing understanding of a different tribal background. The students determine where they will go in life based on a deep respect for where they come from.

In the classroom, the teaching philosophy invites students to take ownership of their learning. In primary school, the girls were responsible for helping to provide for the basic needs of their families—getting water, helping on the farm, cleaning and looking

The name "Kisaruni" was given to WE Charity's group of secondary schools for its meaning in the two most prominent local languages. For the Kipsigis, kisaru *means "to save." For the Maasai,* kisaruni *describes the act of running somewhere safe. The high school campuses are a safe place for girls and boys to access quality education. From left to right: Mark Nyamasege (Grade 10), Elian Kantai (Grade 12), Nelson Mandela Mereru (Grade 11) and Hincy Muthoni (Grade 11).*

Kisaruni valedictorian Milcah Chepkirui graduated in December 2018 with plans to study medicine.

> **"Being in Kisaruni has been a life-changing experience. Some of us came here when we were shy but had big dreams for our futures, and now we are graduating as confident ladies, full of self-fulfillment."**

after younger siblings—as well as homework. At school, the girls are responsible for enriching their minds and growing as individuals. Teachers are called "educational facilitators" and students are called "learners" to illustrate the importance of active learning. Custom-made desks easily fit together into a hexagon shape, promoting group work and peer-to-peer knowledge sharing. The students encourage and challenge each other as they tap into their potential.

The campus resources are superior to any in the surrounding area. The library is outfitted with African and international authors, beanbag chairs, and a long study table. The big windows provide lots of outdoor light and invite learners to curl up and read. There are countless clubs and sports teams. Even though this is a region where you struggle for cell phone signal, the school has a fully equipped science lab and computer room. The school has even hosted astronomy workshops, where students use a telescope for the first time to identify the stars that guided their ancestors.

Milcah Chepkirui, tutored in the evenings by her mother when she couldn't afford high school, received a full scholarship to the all-girls campus of KGS in 2014. Her favorite subject was biology, and over four years she became an all-star member of the science club and a go-to mentor. Milcah's exemplary academics, friendly nature and confidence in public speaking earned her a special honor on graduation day.

The girl who almost didn't attend high school was selected as the 2018 valedictorian, graduating with plans to pursue a medical degree. Wearing the official black gown and cap, Milcah looked out at her proud parents, her classmates—all unlikely graduates— and their parents, community leaders, her teachers, WE Charity staff, and the donors who made it possible. "Being in Kisaruni has been a life-changing experience," she said confidently in English (her third language). "Some of us came here when we were shy but had big dreams for our futures, and now we are graduating as confident ladies, full of self-fulfillment."

The young women are not only the first girls in their families to go to high school, they are also *graduating* high school. Armed with diplomas, they are a generation of highly educated critical thinkers who are empowered to make change in their own communities and the world.

ZEDDY KOSGEI AND WANDA O'BRIEN

TOP: *As of 2020, over 270 girls have graduated from Kisaruni Group of Schools.*
ABOVE LEFT: *Kisaruni valedictorian Milcah Chepkirui addresses hundreds of people on graduation day.*
ABOVE RIGHT: *Milcah's mother, Ann, congratulates her daughter. Ann was one of the few women in her village to have a primary education and was determined to see her daughter succeed.*

A new mark of manhood

In Maasai tradition, boys become men by bringing home a lion's mane. But this young warrior is fighting for a new prize: a high school diploma.

Francis Naimodu was five years old when he became a shepherd, barely taller than the creatures in his care. His father had just died, and while his older brother Peter became head of the household and looked after younger siblings, Francis found work guarding sheep to help sustain the family. For two years he lived alone with his flock, far from his village of Esinoni. He milked the sheep and made porridge with the flour his employer brought him once a week. And during storms, he brought the lambs into his small shelter to keep them healthy, just as Peter had instructed.

Older, stronger boys wielded wooden clubs to defend their flocks. Francis had only his wits and the few materials he scavenged from the village. Armed with a handful of wires, battery cells and a bulb affixed to scrap wood, Francis faced the hyenas that stalked the rural plains. At nightfall he switched on his homemade torch, which gave his slight frame a looming presence.

Peter marveled at his little brother's ingenuity. He knew that Francis had the potential to become a strong Maasai leader, that he could change the lives of his family and likely his entire village. But for boys of their tribe, the path forward was less clear than it used to be. Maasai traditions were changing. Men once gained warrior status by killing a lion or performing a daring cattle raid, but the community no longer supported those practices. "People don't want to fight anymore," Peter explained. "They know that the only way out is education."

Francis would undergo a different rite of passage, one that reflected the realities of a new generation of Maasai. Peter brought Francis home from the plains, and with his brother's earnings he purchased school supplies and a uniform and enrolled him in Grade 1 at Esinoni Primary, a WE Charity partner school. He tasked Francis with becoming the first in their family to bring home a diploma. "If you don't step forward, you will always remain in the same place," Peter told him.

PILLAR

★ **EDUCATION**

Francis Naimodu: former shepherd, aspiring engineer

From his first days in primary school, Francis carried his lessons back to his family. He urged Peter to plant Napier grass, which better sustained the cows, a trick he'd learned in agriculture class. He rigged wires to create a lighting system around the homestead, keeping their animals secure at night. And when neighbors asked Francis to fix their broken radios for a small fee, he used the money to buy books for his younger siblings.

In 2016, Francis completed Grade 8 with good grades and a clear vision: he wanted to build things—to become an engineer. But with very little family income and few high schools in the area, this mission would be harder than hunting big game.

Francis had heard about WE Charity in primary school but knew little of the organization beyond its name. He didn't know that it works to remove barriers that keep children like him from reaching their goals. And he didn't know the organization had previously opened an all-girls high school in the region, as part of its Kisaruni Group of Schools. But when Peter brought him the news that Kisaruni would be opening its first all-boys campus in 2017, and that acceptance guaranteed a full scholarship, Francis knew precisely what he had to do. He applied to the new boys' high school alongside 385 other candidates, vying for a spot in its inaugural class. And just like his childhood invention, his promise shone through, securing him one of 33 coveted places.

At age 13 Francis left home once again, this time headed for the boys' campus in the verdant Ngulot Hills. Though he knew the road ahead would not be as perilous as the plains he had roamed as a child, Peter's words still gave him strength and comfort: "Whether life is difficult or easy, let us go through it and work to change our destiny."

Following his first year of high school, Francis joined the father-son mentorship program, where older students ("fathers") mentor the new class ("sons") by helping them adjust to campus life. For Francis it was an opportunity to pass on the guidance he had received from his own father figure, Peter, and build his skills as a leader. With the new flock under his care, he shared a treasured Maasai saying: "If you step somewhere no one has stepped before, you will create your own mark."

DEEPA SHANKARAN

FACING PAGE: *Peter Naimodu, Francis's older brother and champion*
ABOVE: *Maasai elders from WE Charity's partner communities encourage the younger generation to pursue an education but also to remember their roots. The Kisaruni Group of Schools curriculum reinforces cultural and community connections.*

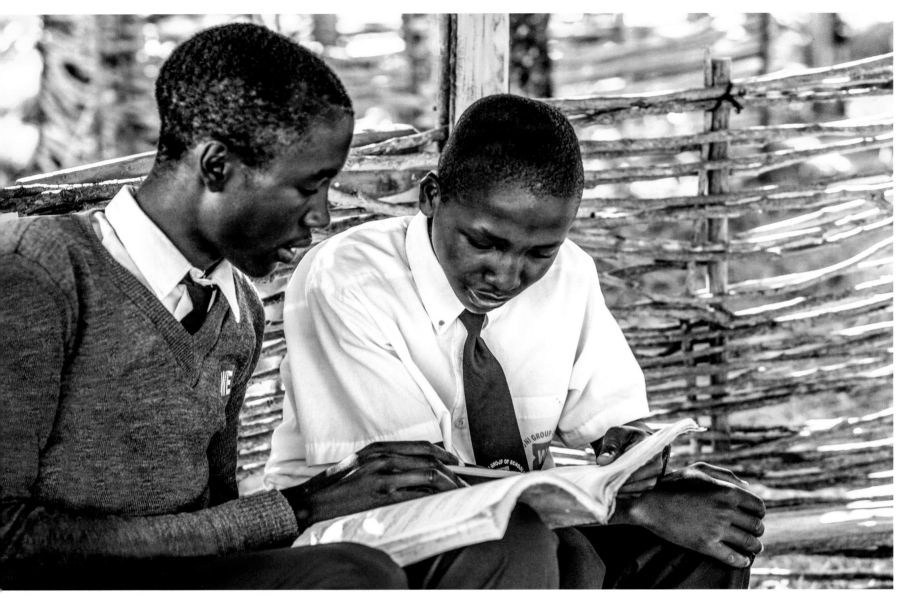

Group studying is a key component of the school's philosophy of "active learning."
Students consult with their peers during designated homework time to wrestle through
challenges and learn new material.

FACING PAGE: *Francis is paired with Grade 9 student Zadock Kibet in a mentorship*
program designed to ease the transition into campus life.

A college rises out of the savanna

PILLAR: EDUCATION

In a region where sturdy primary schools were once a novelty and quality high schools near impossible to find, WE College has opened its doors. Founded for high school graduates from Narok County and beyond, it is the next evolution in educational opportunities that WE Charity offers.

When WE Charity started to work in the region, it focused on improving primary education by bolstering school infrastructure, rebuilding or outfitting rural classrooms and supporting teacher and leadership training. The next step was to help Grade 8 graduates access high school, which can be too expensive for rural families to afford. WE Charity created the Kisaruni Group of Schools in the Maasai Mara, with an all-girls campus and an all-boys campus, which offers full scholarships so that students can continue their education.

Long before the first crop of Kisaruni high school graduates started to contemplate job prospects, WE Charity's country staff were busy mapping out potential trajectories. The majority of colleges and universities in Kenya are in big cities. Funding and parental concerns about the long distance often prevented rural students, especially girls, from pursuing post-secondary options.

With a groundswell of support from donors who believed in the transform-ative potential of education, WE Charity established WE College in 2017. Grade 12 graduates can now access post-secondary opportunities in a deeply rural context, an impossibility just a few years ago.

Located within a cluster of WE Charity partner communities, the college offers full scholarships in accredited programs to specifically meet local needs and industry demands. WE College first opened the School of Tourism, within the Faculty of Technical Studies, and the School of Nursing, within the Faculty of Public Health. Every program includes an internship placement, customized leadership courses, and integration with the computer lab and technology hub so students can acquire skills that will provide a competitive advantage for meaningful employment. As it evolves, the college will offer courses in business, technology, education, medicine and civil engineering.

WE College students come from across the country, but many are from local communities and were once the first in their families to go to high school—some even the first to complete their primary education. Within a single generation, these young leaders have closed a historical education gap. There's no telling where their dreams will lead.

The first class of the School of Nursing on the steps of WE College

This is where my dream becomes my reality

At every hurdle, Alice remained focused and steadfast. WE Charity founded WE College to give rural students an opportunity they wouldn't readily come by otherwise.

Alice Macharia looked up at the big blue gates and read the sign in white lettering: "WE." Until the previous day, she had never heard of WE. As she made her way onto its new campus to fill out a college application, she realized every decision she'd ever made had led to this moment. How she answered the questions in front of her would determine her future—whether she would resign herself to marriage or become the first person in her family to go to college.

She started to write.

Less than 1 percent of college students in Kenya come from Narok County, the region where Alice lives and where WE Charity works. And fewer than half of those students are girls. This is the story of one girl's determination to defy the status quo and WE Charity's commitment to helping a generation of young Kenyan women succeed.

Primary possibilities

Living in the village of Melili, Alice maintained a meticulous routine that was the difference between success and failure in primary school. As the eldest child in a family headed by a single mother, she was responsible for her two younger sisters before and after school, while her mom worked for wealthier families. Alice also cleaned the house, spent two hours making trips to the Narok River to fetch water, and made dinner every night. She only lay down to sleep once the house was in order and she had a plan for what she needed to study the next morning. She'd wake at 5 a.m. and do her homework by the light of a kerosene lamp, until it was time to rouse her sisters. She'd feed them breakfast, which had to sustain them until dinner, then they'd set out for school.

By the age of 10, Alice was spending Saturdays helping her mom wash clothes or working alongside her as a farm laborer. Her mom worked six days each week, using the earnings to pay rent and keep her daughters clothed, fed and in school. Having graduated from Grade 8, Alice's mom believed her daughters needed more education than she had if they were to have any chance of escaping poverty.

PILLAR

★ EDUCATION

Alice Macharia: daughter, planner, top performer

137

Alice used to ask her teachers for extra homework in math and science. She found these subjects challenging but knew they were essential for her future career in nursing.

"I had to bring everything that was in my mind to paper. I told them about my passion for nursing, that I wanted to help people. I just needed a chance."

"She used to ask me, 'Do you want books or food?'" recalls Alice. As the eldest child, she was expected to set an example for her sisters by doing well on the Grade 8 national exams that determined the quality of high school she could attend and, ultimately, her future.

Two months before the exam, Alice's mom took over the task of fetching water to give her daughter more time to study, while Alice awoke an hour earlier to have more time with her books. The extra effort paid off. Alice scored near the top of her class and was accepted into a well-reputed public girls' high school in the area. As planned, Alice would be the first in her family to go to secondary school.

High school hopes

The prospect of high school posed its own challenge. Although Alice had been accepted into a public school, all the additional costs were more than her family could afford. She asked aunts and uncles, friends and neighbors for loans, but couldn't raise enough money. She took on as much work as she could find, even sorting through garbage for glass bottles to earn KSh100 (US$1) a day. "I had to find a way to go back to school," Alice says simply. Her commitment inspired members of the local church, who banded together to cover Alice's school fees for all four years. She started high school imagining life's possibilities: "I thought, what kind of person do I want to be in the future?"

The answer came when she was at home on a school break in Grade 10. Her cousin had a severe asthma attack and Alice sprang into action, loosening her cousin's collar, helping her to focus on breathing, shouting for help. "It hit me," Alice recalls. "I felt it. I want to help people." She wanted to be a nurse.

Alice applied to four college programs. The Kenya Medical Training College was her top choice. "People really expected much of me. I had to do this for myself and my family," she says. She wrote her final high school exams in November 2015, applying the same discipline and rigor that had brought her that far.

Alice was at her part-time dishwasher job when the news broke on the restaurant's television that the results had been posted. She left her shift early to check her marks. She'd done it! Scoring third in her class, she was guaranteed acceptance to the college of her choice. Then she learned the cost of tuition. Her excitement turned to despair. Alice had to let her spot go.

For the next two years, she worked tirelessly but hopefully as a day laborer on nearby farms, a dishwasher and a clothes washer. She collected and sold glass bottles. But the tuition was still out of reach. "I would go home and cry myself to sleep. I was asking myself, 'Why me? Why am I not getting any money to go to school?' It's either that or maybe I go look for a man to marry me, because I didn't have anything else to do with my life."

College aspirations

On one of those difficult days, a neighbor came to Alice's home bursting with news. Not only did she have a newborn to show off, she was also eager to share that she'd given birth at Baraka Hospital, a facility almost four hours away built by WE Charity. The organization was opening a college beside the hospital, with full scholarships for nursing students. This was the best news of all—at least from Alice's perspective.

Alice's resolute spirit flared. Early the following morning, she set off to find Baraka Hospital. She took a three-hour public bus ride past a town called Mulot, arriving at the unmarked intersection her neighbor had told her about. She got on the back of a motorcycle taxi and swerved around countless potholes on a dirt road. Finally, she arrived in front of the blue gates marked with the word "WE."

The nursing program application took her two hours to fill out. "This was my time," Alice recalls. "I had to bring everything that was in my mind to paper. I told them about my passion for nursing, that I wanted to help people. I just needed a chance."

After giving them her mother's cell phone number, Alice made the long journey home, afraid to hope. And even when the call came, inviting her back for a formal interview, she still didn't believe her luck had turned.

During the interview, Alice explained how hard her mother worked to put her children through school, and how that had inspired Alice to be a role model for her younger siblings. She talked about how she wanted to become a nurse and work with mothers and children in her own community.

A week after the interview, two years after completing her high school exams, Alice received a formal acceptance into the School of Nursing at WE College, along with a full scholarship. Alice screamed, fell to her knees and started to cry. She wasn't alone. Her mom was crying too.

Alice and 17 other women joined WE College as its inaugural nursing class in November 2017. Each one is the first in her family to go to college. "Getting a chance to go to college brings dignity to my family. Being a nurse in the community means you are very respected," Alice says. "This is where my dream becomes my reality."

WANDA O'BRIEN

Alice adjusts the IV fluid flow during her nursing residency at Narok's Longisa Hospital in 2019. Once she graduates from WE College, Alice plans to work in pediatric care, serving the community where she grew up.

Rose's journey from charcoal to chicken coop

In rural Kenya, female farmers become first-time entrepreneurs with an investor base that is determined to see success: each other.

Rose Mutai's commute time came close to a typical workday—seven hours one-way to the charcoal depot, where her true labor began. She'd wake before dawn, before the kids dressed for school, before her husband left for the corn fields. Too early to light a fire and make tea for her children, she'd stealthily dress in the dark, wrap her shoulders in a *kanga* to keep out the cold, and then go.

No streetlight lit the worn path of trampled grass from her rural home in Kipsongol to the nearest paved road. Muscle memory guided her way. And even when the conductor hung out of a passing *matatu* hustling fares, she'd wave him away—no money for a bus.

She'd arrive at the depot by 11 a.m. to collect charcoal to sell along the roadside to other rural Kenyans who relied on it for fuel. As late afternoon fell, she'd start the long journey home. Everything Rose did was to ensure that her six children could one day go to high school and surpass her own Grade 8 education.

Before having children, Rose and her husband were farmers, selling what they could from their one-acre plot. But with each new child, the expenses grew. Although primary school is mandatory in Kenya, parents are charged for maintenance, repair fees and sometimes salaries for teachers. For low-income farmers, paying the average KSh400 (US$4) per term is challenging. By the time a child reaches high school, the cost of uniforms, books and school supplies is thousands of shillings per term. A child's education slips out of reach without a parent's unwavering determination and hustle.

Twice a week, Rose spent 19 hours per day collecting and selling charcoal, unable to find any other way to meet her family's needs. "I had no other options," Rose reflects, speaking Swahili. "Once my kids started growing up, they needed to go to school, so we had to find a way."

We sit in her living room on a wooden bench adorned with worn cushions, chai perched on our laps. She promises to tell me how a charcoal laborer became a successful businesswoman. I hang on to every word, keen to understand her resilience and her story.

PILLARS

 OPPORTUNITY

 EDUCATION

Rose Mutai: mother, hostess, entrepreneur
FOLLOWING SPREAD: *Rose stands in front of her property. The chicken coop she built using start-up funds from her women's group is in the background (left).*

ABOVE: *Neighbor Elizabeth Ngerechi, a member of another opportunity group in Kipsongol, passes by the Tech Gaa meeting and inquires about the group's activities.*

FACING PAGE: *When Emily Tuwei became a new mom to baby Bethwel, her women's group bought her a care package of sugar, tea leaves, soap and baby clothes.*

As Rose's family grew, so did her connections to other women. Whenever a baby was born in the village, neighbors would bring handmade blankets, soap, tea leaves and sugar to ease the pressure of caring for a newborn. Over time, with Rose at the helm, the women began to meet monthly, whether or not there was a new baby to celebrate—the camaraderie found over soft, warm *mandazi*s (local fried dough) and steaming chai were reason enough to gather. But there weren't enough cups to go around, so it was BYOC (bring your own cup) whenever the women met.

"When I'd have visitors, I'd ask for the other mamas to help me out, if I could borrow a cup and plate," Rose explains. "Eventually we said, 'Enough! We can't continue borrowing each other's plates and cups. We need our own.'"

In 2013, Rose and seven other women formalized their gatherings and founded the Tech Gaa women's group. It means "build your home" in Rose's first language, Kipsigis. The women started a variation of a savings club known as a merry-go-round, which are popular in East Africa. But at first it wasn't money the women were collecting, but the housewares necessary to become better hostesses.

In typical merry-go-rounds, each woman makes a small deposit on a regular basis into a group pot. Once each month the group provides the lump sum to one woman—no strings attached, no need to pay anything back, except the expectation that she will continue to be part of the community and support the other members. But Rose and her friends didn't bring cash to the gathering, they brought hostess gifts—household items such as cups and plates that sold for KSh20 (US$0.20) at the local market. Within the year, Rose had a full set of dinner plates, with enough cups to serve chai to the whole group.

The monthly tea parties were an occasion to show off their upgraded wares, but the group's ambition stalled. "Cups and plates," Rose says with a laugh and a shrug. "That's all we ever did." The women didn't yet see how their small group could become an investment source to change each other's lives.

Rose continued the long walk twice a week to sell charcoal, so she could send her eldest daughter to high school and keep two of her sons in the local elementary school, which WE Charity was helping to rebuild. The charitable organization also planned to drill a borehole to provide clean water to the school as it partnered with the community to put its five-pillar sustainable development model into action, providing education, clean water, health care, food security and economic opportunity.

Then in 2015, WE Charity gave a presentation about financial management, budgeting and leadership skills. Rose was in the audience, raptly listening. She learned that income opportunity would enable true self-sufficiency.

"*Nilifurahi sana*," Rose shares in Swahili, once again laughing at the memory. "I was so happy. I said, 'Come, come to our group, and see how you can help us!'"

A WE Charity mobilizer visited Rose's group to assess its needs. The mobilizer told them that even the KSh20 they used to equip a different hostess with housewares each month would be significant when pooled together. So instead of cups and saucers, the women of Tech Gaa began to bring hard-earned cash to gatherings, starting with KSh20 each. Each month's hostess could use the money as she saw fit.

"We learned from WE Charity that we could buy things that could benefit people in the long term, like goats and chickens," Rose says. The group discussed how to save as a collective to fund individual goals: what they wanted to achieve with start-up funds. The monthly meetings took on weighted significance as the women began to contribute more money, but always with the same tone—women supporting women to "build the home."

Rose's long-held dream was to own a chicken business. "It's a fast way to make money," she explains, ever pragmatic. "You don't have to wait long to make money with chickens. They lay eggs. You can sell the eggs; you can sell the chickens."

A new protocol was put into place. Instead of simply giving the hostess a pool of money each month, with no need to pay it back, the group turned their merry-go-round into a Village Savings and Loan Association (VSLA)—a way to manage money in places where there's no ATM or teller in sight. The friends were running an informal bank. Thirteen more women asked to join, seeing the opportunity to save and access loans for the first time. But it wasn't without trepidation.

"The first month there wasn't enough for someone to buy goats or anything else, so the money was just sitting there," Rose says. "That was hard. And also, we didn't trust each other very well in the beginning. What if we give our money and someone runs off with it?"

The group established checks and balances and came to trust each other. They elected a president and a secretary. Rose was voted treasurer. A mobile safe, with three locks, each with a separate key, provided security. At the end of each meeting, the collected money was carefully counted in front of the group and placed in the metal box. As treasurer, Rose held a key, along with the president and one other group member. All three keys were required to open the safe.

Staff members from WE Charity taught the women to budget and track money. The group learned about loans and microfinance—how the collective pool of money could support each other's ambitions, with time frames and agreed-upon interest rates to pay the loan back into the group's pot for reinvestment.

In 2016, the women started to finance their dreams. Rose borrowed her first

The group turned their merry-go-round into a Village Savings and Loan Association—a way to manage money in places where there's no ATM or teller in sight.

KSh5,000 to buy wire mesh to surround the chicken coop she planned to build on her farm. She knew the wire mesh was essential to keep her investment safe. She started to build the wooden coop while still collecting charcoal twice a week, as she worked toward launching her new venture. Group member Gloria took out a loan to buy a sewing machine to start a tailoring business, Anna bought a piece of land to grow corn, and Karen took a loan to help purchase a dairy cow.

"That's when we realized this can do something, and do something big," Rose remembers. "We became more comfortable."

In 2017, after repaying her first loan, Rose took out a new KSh5,500 to purchase 14 chickens. She sold corn to buy 14 more. With a full flock in her coop, Rose triumphantly quit her trek for charcoal to devote her time and energy to her start-up. She was, and is, all eggs in.

The Tech Gaa group brings together women who live on farms stretched across the community of Kipsongol. They made matching headscarves and skirts in green, the group's official color, to wear to group meetings. From left to right: Ann Bwalei, Betty Sigei and Alice Sin'goei.

Group members show off the cash they will deposit to fund each other's ventures—including sewing machines for tailoring businesses, land to grow cash crops, and goats or cows for animal husbandry.

TOP ROW, FROM LEFT TO RIGHT: *Rose Mutai, Karen Langat, Betty Rotich, Faith Kenduiywa and Ann Bwalei*

The meetings continue—whether in a woman's living room or outside under the shade of a tree. Four empty buckets are always placed on a table between the women. The pink bucket is for savings—what the women will deposit that day. The black one is for loan repayment. The original spirit of Tech Gaa is held in the green bucket, designated for "social" uses. This is money that is spent on gifts for new moms, urgent school fees or helping out with the funeral arrangements for a member's family.

Finally, there is a yellow bucket for fines—KSh10 for being late to meetings or if a mama's phone rings (it happens more than you would think and helps fund the social pot).

"I wanted to improve my home, build my home," Rose explains. Setting aside her teacup, she gestures to the surroundings, the cow grazing outside her front door, along with her chickens, and to the path, where her kids will be arriving home soon from school. "My thinking has been expanded. I realize I can actually do more than farm my small farm at home. I can have a business."

Rose regularly sells eggs to neighbors, and her hens are an insurance policy for any unexpected costs. Her friends are a fortified customer base for each new start-up: women supporting women to become first-time entrepreneurs. Rose has enough for school fees, savings and loan repayment—and is filled with joyful pride as she gives me a tour of her property, her hands no longer streaked with charcoal but carrying freshly laid eggs.

WANDA O'BRIEN

FOLLOWING SPREAD: *As group treasurer, Rose counts the money deposited into the savings bucket before putting it into a lockbox for safekeeping.*

Single share value (Thamani ya Hisa)	Ksh. 100
Cycle Number (Mzunguko wa :-)	003

Date (Tarehe)	Shares bought per meeting				
16/04/2017	100	100	100	100	—
23/04/2017	100	100	100	—	—
15/05/2017	100	100	100	100	—
19/06/2017	100	100	100	—	—

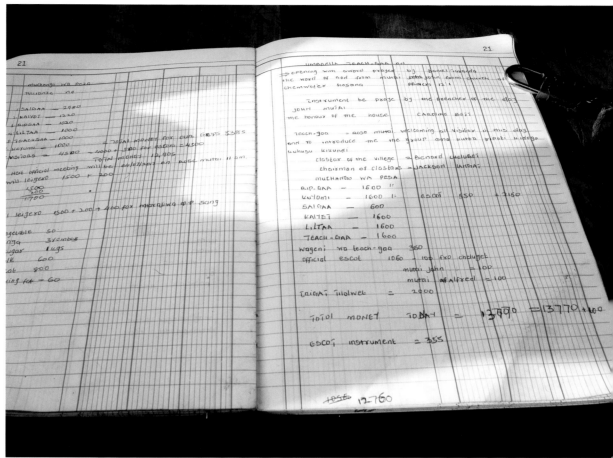

Each deposit is meticulously counted and recorded in the group ledger. In the early stages of the group, WE Charity team members provided training on accounting and budget tracking. Now the group is entirely self-sufficient and runs its own meetings.

TOP LEFT: Ann Bwalei, the group's chairwoman, used loans to invest in chickens and goats.
BOTTOM RIGHT: Secretary Karen Langat tracks the deposits of the day.

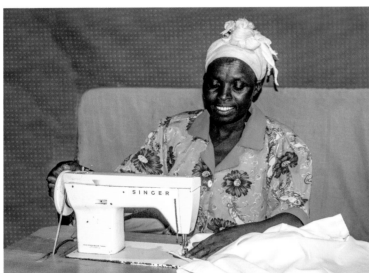

Rose makes a tidy profit selling chickens and eggs. She took out another loan to buy a sewing machine. As she grows her farm and tailoring business, her desire to educate her six children fuels her entrepreneurial spirit. She stands with her sons who attend Kipsongol Primary School, Grade 6 student Phineas (left) and Grade 8 student Gideon (center).

Building a blessing

Key milestones mark the evolution of WE Charity's program to bring quality, affordable health care to rural communities in Kenya. Built out of a need, this is how Baraka Hospital came to life.

A good doctor listens to a patient and then tailors treatment to needs. WE Charity's health pillar works the same way. Health coordinators traveled from village to village and spoke with families, understood their ailments, and responded to what they heard and saw. While their first efforts focused on health education to prevent illness, the team also faced heart-wrenching realities—people who couldn't access urgent treatment.

There was the mama who cut her leg working on her farm and never went to get the wound properly cleaned and stitched. By the time she hobbled up to a WE Charity mobile clinic, the cut had festered into a crippling infection. Other examples abound: the father whose hypertension went untreated for years because of prohibitive travel costs, and who sought medical treatment only after suffering a stroke; the child whose parents didn't know where to go for immunizations; the pregnant woman who didn't recognize the danger signs of complications putting her and the baby at risk.

As WE Charity worked in partnership with communities through its five-pillar model to address the issues keeping people in poverty—access to education, clean water, income opportunities, food security and health programming—the need for a large-scale health intervention was omnipresent, as was the desire for this service from the surrounding communities. With support from champion donors, WE Charity embarked on a journey to create long-term sustainable solutions to people's health care needs in a rural region. It built what would become a center for health excellence known throughout Narok County and beyond: Baraka Hospital. In addition, WE Charity opened Kishon Health Centre to provide preventative health care, as well as specialized services in ophthalmology, dental care and dialysis for renal patients.

The following milestones showcase the history of Baraka from a fateful wheelbarrow ride to the opening of a state-of-the-art operating room. Throughout every development and new initiative, WE Charity's health mandate has remained stable and simple: to make quality health care accessible to all.

PILLAR

❤ HEALTH

Baraka Hospital was born out of a need to serve mothers and children.

Moment 1
The wheelbarrow

2008

Amidst a frenzy of dust along an unpaved road, more than a dozen women shepherded a rusted wheelbarrow carrying precious cargo as they eyed the horizon for help. When a WE Charity field truck approached, they flagged it down. The dust settled. The crowd parted to reveal a woman sitting in the makeshift wheelchair, nine months pregnant and in labor.

Her neighbors had planned to push her several miles to the main road so she could board a public bus and travel another hour to the closest hospital. Her labor pains were so intense she couldn't walk, and riding on the back of a motorbike to the hospital was out of the question. The women eased Mama K* into the truck. WE Charity staff rushed her to the hospital, where she gave birth to a healthy son.

Mama K's plight symbolized the extreme lack of access to quality medical care for people, especially mothers and infants, in rural areas of Narok County in 2008. As WE Charity would learn, Mama K wasn't the only person forced to rely on a wheelbarrow for transport in moments of crisis. Her case, in fact, was not exceptional. In addition to the urgent need for maternal health care, WE Charity staff continued to see families lose loved ones to communicable diseases—where medical intervention would have saved lives.

The idea for Baraka Hospital took hold.

* *Names have been withheld to protect patient privacy.*

Baraka Hospital runs a weekly Child Welfare Clinic where children under five receive government-mandated immunizations and are monitored to make sure they hit developmental milestones. Prevention and health education are core components of WE Charity's health pillar.

Moment 2
What's in a name?

2010

When WE Charity approached community leaders with the idea of a health care center, the response was overwhelming. Elders, parents, headmasters and teachers from the surrounding area eagerly joined in the planning. They wanted to build an inviting space—an extension of the community—providing care to anyone who needed it, where the staff would speak local languages and the interior wouldn't feel cold and clinical. They wanted a center that would provide high-quality care to rural communities, with a focus on women and children. Patients would pay a subsidized fee to use the clinic, but no one would be turned away because of financial constraints.

With the mission clear, WE Charity sought government approvals to bring this project to life. Donors who believed in the purpose of the clinic generously provided funds, and WE Charity purchased the land with community input to situate the clinic in Enelerai, close to a primary school and WE Charity's secondary schools.

Plans were underway, but a key question remained: what to call the clinic? The communities chose *baraka*, a Swahili word that means "blessing." They chose Swahili, Kenya's national language, to show that the clinic was meant for all communities, rather than any one of the country's 42 tribes. And they chose "blessing" because it was the only word that summed up how they felt about the project.

In 2010, Baraka Health Center opened as a permanent medical facility, offering treatment to outpatients, prenatal services to expecting mothers, government-mandated immunizations for children, and referral services to nearby hospitals for complex cases. Patients who couldn't afford the doctor's fee still received treatment without delay; they would often return with eggs, a chicken or home-grown kale as a token of appreciation for services received. Once the center opened, another vehicle took to Narok's roads—an ambulance. Pregnant women about to give birth and others with medical emergencies would no longer have to rely on wheelbarrows or motorcycles.

With the first phase of the project complete, the WE Charity team turned their attention to the construction of a maternity ward to provide a safe space for deliveries and newborn care.

The communities chose baraka, *a Swahili word that means "blessing."*

Lab technologist and Baraka Hospital manager Nehemia Kahato helps create an inviting and friendly environment that puts patients at ease. "This is a patient's home whenever they want to seek health care," he says.

Moment 3
A new era of care: the maternity ward

2013

In April 2013, Baraka's maternity ward was inaugurated with the birth of its first baby, a boy. The entire Baraka team, even those who were off duty, rushed to the clinic to celebrate. The next baby born was a girl, with her twin sister following 20 minutes later. The number of births continued to increase month over month as word spread about the maternity ward's quality of care. Women who experienced distress during their pregnancies came to Baraka for help.

Baraka receives a high volume of patients through word-of-mouth referrals. Patients often cite the attentiveness of staff, cleanliness of the facilities and first-rate resources as reasons for choosing Baraka.

One of those women was Mama C. After seven successful home births, the 36-year-old mother felt something wasn't normal when she went into labor with her eighth child. More than 14 hours into the labor, unsure of what was happening, she went to the recently opened maternity ward at Baraka Health Center. After an assessment, Mama C was informed her unborn boy was in a posterior position—face up rather than face down. The situation was not life-threatening but it was causing the delay. The staff set up to monitor Mama C, hoping she would be able to deliver routinely. But after another five hours of labor, it was time for action. A Baraka clinician successfully changed the position of the baby, who was born soon after at a healthy 8.1 pounds.

Within the first year, 78 babies were born in Baraka's maternity ward. Every year that number continued to increase. But there were unmet challenges. In the event of complications requiring a caesarean section, women were transferred by ambulance to a local hospital. The Baraka team was still not equipped to perform surgeries. Another evolution in care was about to begin.

Baraka was conceived as a community blessing, but members are passing on their own blessings after going there.

Three generations: a first-time mother gazes down at her baby girl, who was delivered by emergency C-section and rests in the arms of her grandmother.

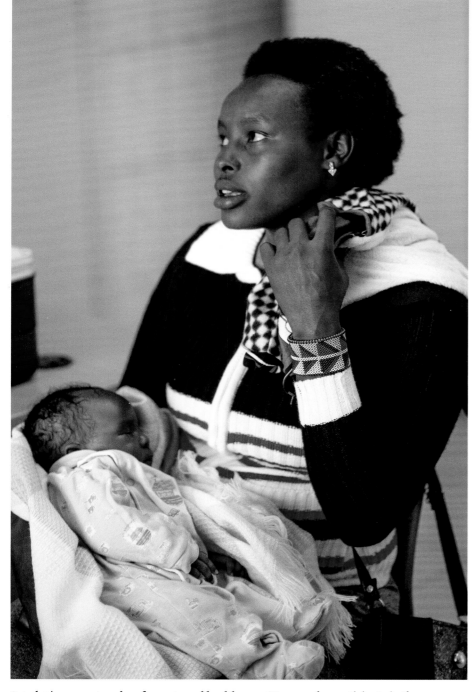

Baraka is a one-stop shop for maternal health care. Women who participate in the prenatal clinic also deliver at the maternity ward and seamlessly transition into postnatal services for themselves and their newborns.

Moment 4
Hospital status

2017

In May 2017, Mama N tried to check into a hospital near Mulot town in Narok County when she went into labor. She was told to go home; the baby wasn't ready to make its debut. She wasn't comfortable with that advice, so the mom-to-be traveled down a dirt road to the gates of the newly certified Baraka Hospital. The surgical unit and inpatient wing had just opened, which elevated the health center to hospital status.

When Mama N arrived at Baraka, she was pushed by wheelchair into the

examination room. The doctor quickly determined that her labor was obstructed and that the situation was critical for both mother and child. The team performed an emergency caesarean section. The very first surgery performed in Baraka Hospital's new operating room resulted in a baby boy being welcomed into the world.

With hospital designation, Baraka's capability and services expanded to include minor and major surgery, and it offered patients more coverage under Kenya's National Hospital Insurance Fund, which provides medical care for Kenyans without private insurance. Nearly 400 babies were born at Baraka in 2017, more than doubling the previous year's record. The reason for the baby boom? Women from distant communities started coming to the hospital, knowing they would receive the best possible attention.

The Baraka Hospital grounds were thoughtfully designed to create a peaceful and welcoming environment.

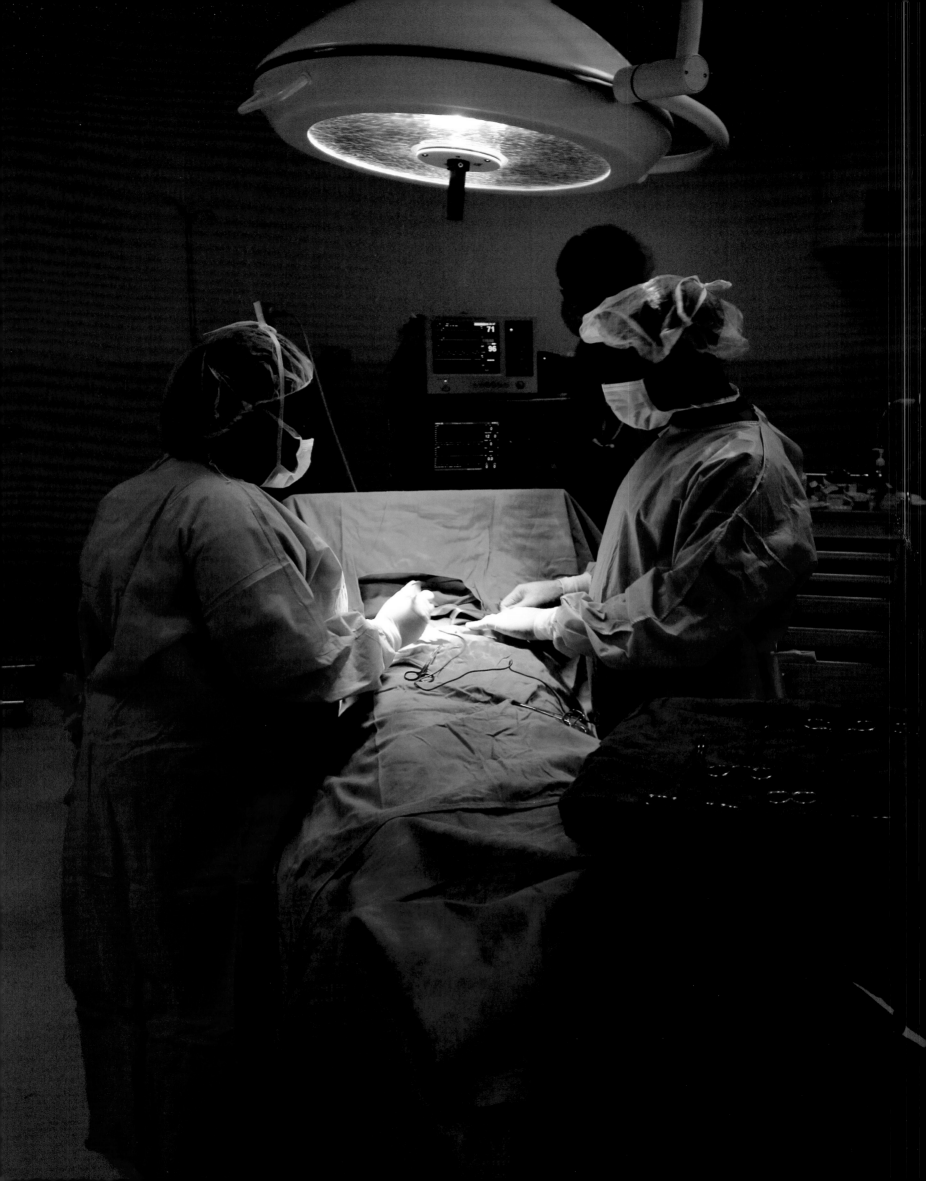

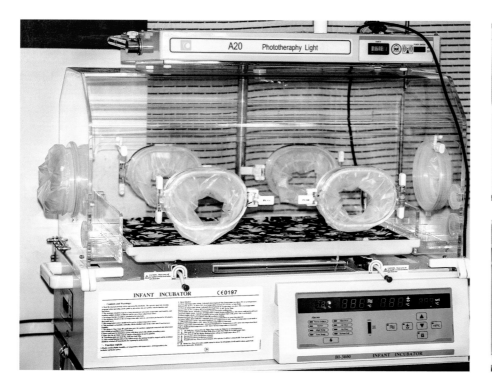

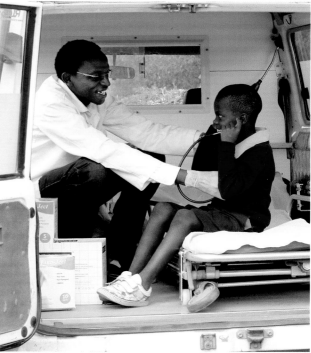

FACING PAGE: *The opening of the surgical unit cemented Baraka Hospital as a primary health care leader in the region.*

TOP LEFT: *The neonatal incubator enables Baraka staff to respond to emergencies within a newborn's first moments of life.*

TOP RIGHT: *Baraka Hospital provides care to patients of all ages, whether at the hospital or through mobile medical clinics.*

ABOVE: *Baraka staff consult with a patient during the Comprehensive Care Clinic that provides services for people who are HIV positive.*

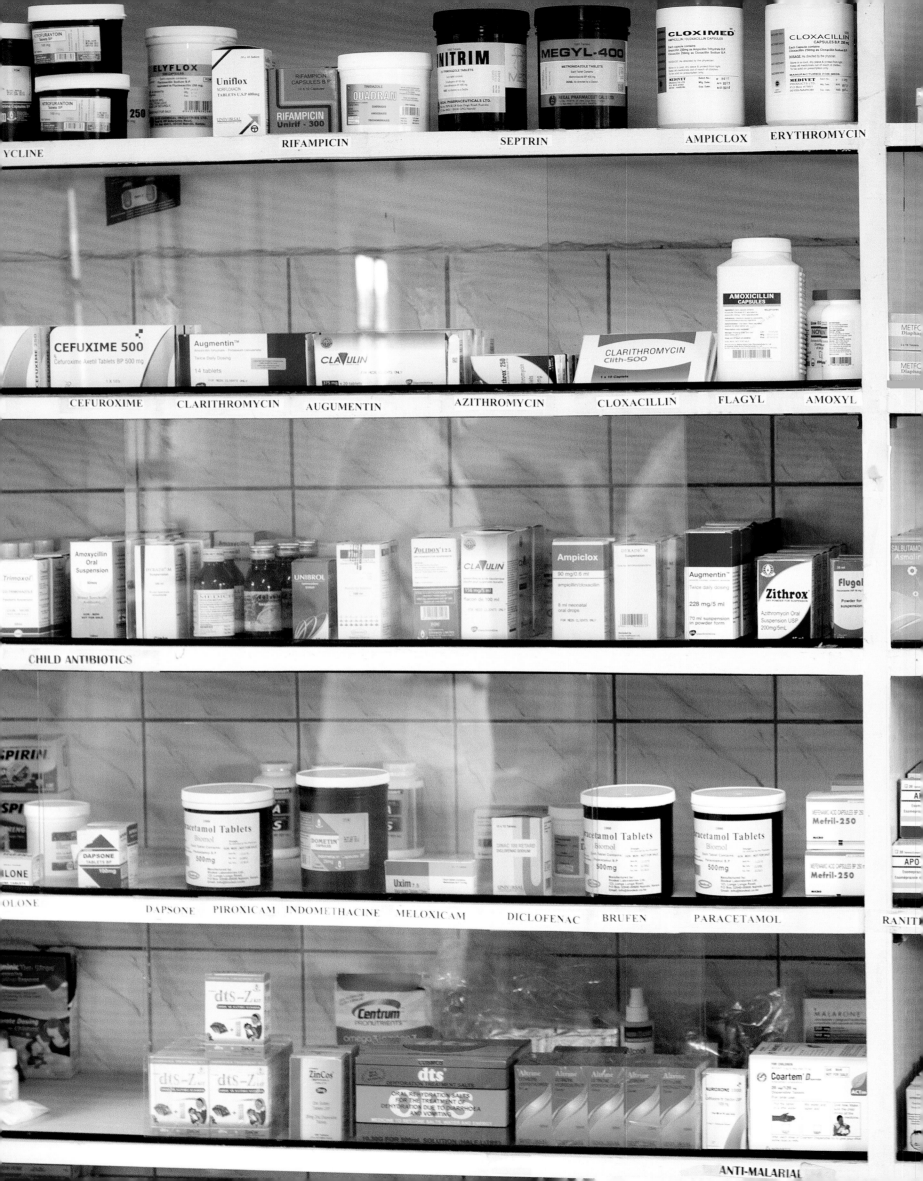

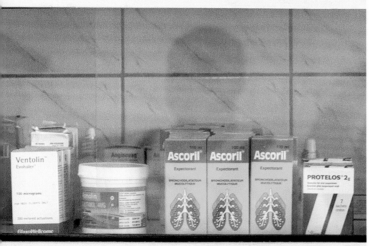

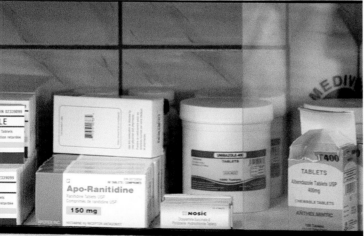

Moment 5
A center for health care excellence
2019

Baraka Hospital is not what you would expect to find down five miles of dirt road in rural Narok County. Yet there it is, a state-of-the-art medical facility that as of 2020 had received more than 90,000 visits.

The Child Welfare Clinic is on Tuesdays, and moms bounce their little ones as they wait to have their development measured, get nutritional and health-related programming support, and receive up-to-date immunizations. On Thursdays, the hospital's lawn is peppered with pregnant mamas waiting their turn at the prenatal clinic to discuss birth plans and receive prenatal vitamins, nutritional supplements and ultrasounds (technology previously unheard of in the area). Every day, as part of ongoing outpatient care, visitors can see a doctor and pick up medications from the hospital's well-stocked pharmacy. As needed, the medical team schedules surgeries that were once out of reach. Specialized programming, such as the comprehensive care program for HIV-positive mothers, attracts people who otherwise would not have a treatment option. The program has achieved a mother-to-child transmission rate of zero.

Baraka is slated to become a teaching hospital by partnering with WE College's Faculty of Public Health. Children who grew up in the area and studied at schools supported by WE Charity will do their medical practicums under this flagship hospital program.

Baraka was conceived as a community blessing, but members are passing on their own blessings after going there. Following the delivery of her second child through an emergency C-section at Baraka, one mama summed it up: *"Kongoi, kongoi missing dagitari. Mungu asaidie waliojenga hii hospitali ambayo imenisaidia."* In English this means: "Thank you, thank you so much, doctor. God bless the people who built the hospital that helped me."

May the blessings continue.

WANDA O'BRIEN

Baraka Hospital serves a catchment area of 67,000 people. With a fully stocked pharmacy, surgical unit, and teams of specialized doctors and surgeons, patients now benefit from health care resources previously unavailable in the underserved region.

Medicine on the move

PILLAR: HEALTH

The Baraka Hospital ambulance hits the road in Narok County fully stocked with life-saving cargo. The team onboard is not out to respond to health emergencies, but rather working to prevent them.

Every week, a nurse and a social worker hold pop-up health clinics in remote WE Charity communities. Villages struggle to access basic medical care; many are located more than a 90-minute drive from WE Charity's medical centers, Baraka Hospital and Kishon Health Centre.

Local WE Charity primary schools become temporary clinic base camps, while community mobilizers and school headmasters spread the word. When the ambulance parks near the school, the singsong voices of children ring out in welcome. A schoolroom is transformed into an outpatient exam room; the schoolyard becomes a makeshift waiting area.

Mothers arrive with their toddlers in tow to receive government-mandated vaccinations, while pregnant women receive prenatal vitamins and health checkups. Community members experiencing pain or sickness seek advice, and treatments for gastrointestinal diseases are doled out. Complex cases are referred to hospitals. And the schoolchildren who sing out in welcome? Every six months they receive deworming medication to prevent parasites that keep them from class. This is a powerful dose of preventative medicine.

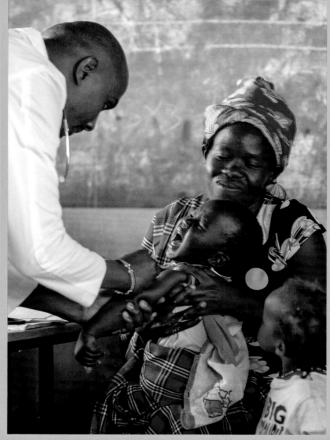

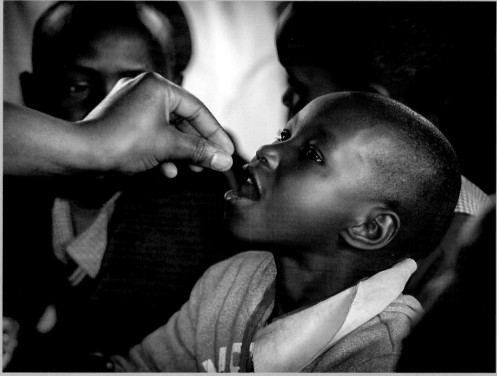

FACING PAGE: *Community members line up for an outpatient clinic at a primary school.*
ABOVE: *Primary-school children in WE Charity partner communities receive deworming pills every six months as part of the organization's health programming in Kenya.*

Mama Jane on being a boss

As a mother, farmer, health advocate, entrepreneur and community leader, Mama Jane is determined to be a role model for her children and, in turn, inspires countless others.

Jane Marindany's ceiling maps her greatest achievements. The homework of her five children has been turned into artwork over many years, the lined pages of their notebooks cut into intricate designs of squares, stars and triangles and then strung from one corner of her living room to the other. To her, this signals her children's academic growth, a tribute to countless hours spent on math equations and geography classes, English lessons and science formulas. It's proof of every grade passed in a house built by Jane's hands—her own great accomplishment.

Mama Jane, as she is affectionately known, is a titan among leaders, a trailblazing lady boss whose family-first approach, work ethic and business prowess transformed her life and the lives of her neighbors.

She was born in Emori Joi, one of the first communities WE Charity partnered with in Kenya's Narok County. Mama Jane not only witnessed her community's transformation as a result of its partnership, she also actively ignited many of the changes. "I was taught first how to be a leader in my own home and family, then how to be a group leader here in my community," she says.

In 2004, WE Charity started to build new classrooms for the primary school and improve access to quality education, later bringing in health, water, alternative income and food security programming. Mama Jane watched as the new classrooms were constructed, and she encouraged her kids to reach beyond her own Grade 4 education.

She lived in a *boma*, a one-room hut made of mud and thatch, with her husband, Julius, and children, and sometimes their goats and sheep. After attending WE Charity's health training, Mama Jane began to transform their home, building a latrine and installing a chimney so her family no longer breathed in smoke when they were inside. She set up an outdoor drying rack and designated a place for handwashing. She hoped to one day build a new house, one that reflected how she'd come to see herself.

PILLARS

♥ HEALTH

☗ OPPORTUNITY

★ EDUCATION

Jane Marindany: woman of influence

Jane's merry-go-round group pooled their savings and invested in goats for each member.

WE Charity's opportunity programming provided training on how to generate more income through the local merry-go-round group, a micro-savings practice common in rural Kenya where there is no access to banking. This provided her with the entrepreneurial know-how to hammer out her dreams.

Each week, Mama Jane and her neighbors brought a small amount of money, KSh50, or about US$0.50, to a meeting. The combined sum was given to a different woman at the end of each meeting with no requirement to pay back the full amount, but with the understanding that each woman would continue to contribute on an ongoing basis. With guidance from WE Charity trainers, the women started to increase their weekly contributions to KSh100, then KSh200 and more. When Mama Jane was elected chairwoman of her merry-go-round circle, she advised the women: "Start small. Don't compare yourself to others and get discouraged. Be patient and consistent and save as much as you can."

TOP: *Jane built a dish-drying rack at home after attending WE Charity health training, where she learned that drying dishes in the sunlight helps keep them bacteria-free. The training promotes small changes that make a big difference in the health of families.*

ABOVE: *Nancy Tangus, Jane's friend and neighbor, lights her stove. She installed a chimney to channel smoke out of her home, on the advice of WE Charity's health mobilizer.*

RIGHT: *Nancy is part of a dairy cooperative with over 500 micro-entrepreneurs who sell their cows' milk to a mainstream market.*

ABOVE: *Jane with her dairy cow, Daisy.*
FACING PAGE: *Nancy picks fodder for cattle feed*

Plans to start a dairy cooperative were developed. More than 500 micro-entrepreneurs across 32 women's groups wanted in.

Soon all the women in the group had built toilets and installed chimneys in their compounds, their health and opportunity training merging together. Other women's groups, also supported by WE Charity, followed suit. Next the groups decided to buy every member chickens, the profits from egg sales going toward school supplies for their children. Then they purchased goats, their kids acting as an insurance policy in times of need. Determined to further finance their futures, the women decided to invest in dairy cows.

In 2010, Mama Jane's group started to buy one dairy cow for every member. It took 24 months. Only after everyone else had one would Mama Jane accept her cow. The women now had milk for their families but nowhere to sell the surplus. Mama Jane consulted her friend Nancy Tangus, chairwoman of another women's group facing a similar predicament. Jane and Nancy, with the support of WE Charity, assembled chairwomen from all the women's groups in the area to discuss how to maximize their earnings.

Jane's new house stands as proof of what is possible.

"I wanted to show my husband and all the men in my community that the small savings from our women's group could build something big."

Plans to start a dairy cooperative were developed. More than 500 micro-entrepreneurs across 32 women's groups wanted in. Mama Jane was elected chairwoman. "All the woman stood up and started singing. I was in shock." They all saw her drive, determination and success. Soon the co-op was generating so much milk they were able to find a wholesaler who in turn helped them tap a larger market. People in urban centers across Kenya were buying cartons of milk from the women's dairy cows. For the first time, the women received a monthly salary.

Slowly but steadily, Mama Jane built her dream house. At first, Julius didn't take her seriously. Only men built concrete houses, he told her. "I wanted to show my husband and all the men in my community that the small savings from our women's group could build something big," recalls Mama Jane, who consulted with a builder and mapped out dimensions. She gradually amassed materials and laid the foundation. Julius saw the progress and started to wake earlier to help his wife with the construction.

After four years, the family moved into their new home, the house that Jane had built. Jane slept late the morning after moving in, reveling in her family's newfound comfort. Her children no longer struggled to find a place to study. And after they passed their exams, their mother hung their homework overhead, a reminder of what's possible with hard work, support and perseverance.

WANDA O'BRIEN

ABOVE LEFT: *Julius, Jane's husband, joined a men's opportunity group created with WE Charity support after seeing the success of his wife's group.*

ABOVE RIGHT: *Growing up, Joyline, Jane's daughter, shared what she learned at school each day with her mom, including teaching her how to spell her name. Joyline graduated from a primary school built by WE Charity and received a scholarship to attend high school at the Kisaruni Group of Schools.*

LEFT: *Jane's property. Her chicken coop sits in front of the one-room boma (pictured in the background) that once housed the whole family but now serves just one function, as the kitchen.*

The fruits (and vegetables) of food security

Carefully crafted interventions help farmers grow enough food to feed their families sustainably, adding cash crops to the harvest for the first time.

By necessity and design, WE Charity's food programming provides much more than a single meal.

In 2011, a drought destroyed farmers' fields across Kenya. The following year, a fungal disease wiped out corn crops—a daily dietary staple in Narok County. To help struggling subsistence farmers become self-reliant and food secure, WE Charity launched its food pillar, the fifth in its five-pillar model.

Ambitious? Yes. Life-changing? Absolutely. Food security means reliable access to nutritious meals on an ongoing basis; it means securing quantity *and* quality. To provide a sustainable solution, WE Charity offered training in seed distribution, soil nutrients, irrigation and post-harvest storage. With coaching, family farms became micro-businesses.

In 2013, Oleleshwa Farm was established as a center for community training and to provide nutritious meals to WE Charity's high school students. At the farm, which spans more than 30 acres, trainees are inspired by the rows of produce bursting from the ground, the impressive lineup of 14 greenhouses protecting more vulnerable vegetables, and the kilos of crop yields collected at harvest time.

Oleleshwa has ignited a passion for agriculture in the next generation. Grade 12 Kisaruni student Elian Kantai joined her high school's agriculture club and learned about crop rotation and drip irrigation during visits to Oleleshwa. When she brought her lessons home, her mother planted tomatoes for the first time, generating extra income through sales.

When Simone Ruto, a father of three young children, received training at Oleleshwa Farm, he marveled at the abundance of diverse crops growing less than an hour from his own listless kale and corn fields. His farm was failing because he lacked access to water. When an agricultural trainer showed him the channels of pipes snaking through the earth at Oleleshwa, drip irrigation for the thirsty crops, Simone saw possibility. When the trainer pointed out the benefits of intercropping, he saw potential.

PILLAR

♦ **FOOD**

Grade 12 student Elian Kantai discovers sustainable farming practices at Oleleshwa Farm.

At home, he dug shallow channels and laid thin pipes to connect his farm to a nearby borehole drilled by WE Charity. For the first time, he planted millet and cabbage seedlings and banana and avocado trees. Within the year, his land was producing varied and hearty harvests; the avocado trees were steadily growing for long-term payoff and he was selling surplus kale and corn.

WE Charity has also developed one-acre farms within seven communities that act as incubators for new crops and safe spaces to try new farming methods. The farms are run by community volunteers who split the produce and profits grown from their collective efforts. Then they take their agricultural acumen to their personal plots. WE Charity's food pillar is rooted in sustainability that will serve the health and well-being of families for generations.

WANDA O'BRIEN

ABOVE: *A row of greenhouses inspires subsistence farmers to diversify their crops. Tomatoes, cucumbers and peppers grow throughout the year.*
LEFT: *Simone Ruto stands proudly with his son in front of his improved kale crop.*
FACING PAGE: *At Oleleshwa Farm, WE Charity specialists train farmers in how to improve their crops, and they provide high school students with knowledge and skills to take home to their parents' fields.*

The secret to winning

The Melelo income-opportunity groups chose their names as self-fulfilling prophecies. The women and men of each group invest in each other to positively impact their whole community.

More corn. A new sheep. Money to send their kids to school. A cow to come. The women spoke in rapid succession as each expressed the impact that belonging to the micro-savings group had had on her life. Every few sentences, the stream of Maa was broken with the pop of a single English word—"winning"—followed by laughter.

The Winning Group is a WE Charity merry-go-round savings club in the Maasai community of Melelo. As with all WE Charity community groups, the members chose the name. In Maa, the word for winning is *inkatenak*, and although the women play with the English equivalent in conversation, they are serious about the group's intention. "As women, it's important to come together, because we are the ones who see the challenges," Retoe Enole Keiwua, the chairwoman, says in Maa through a translator. "We decided as a group to find things that would improve our lives and raise us up."

Their spirit was infectious. In turn, WE Charity helped the young men in Melelo form a youth group. They named it Nabosho, which means "togetherness," to reflect their mandate. The group sells rams and bulls to cover the costs of younger members' education.

The women's and men's groups have crossover beyond similar mandates. Nailepu Enole Keiwua is a mother of seven whose son Dickson dropped out of high school because she couldn't afford his fees. After joining the Winning Group, Nailepu secured the money to return her son to school. She also encouraged him to join the young men's group. Dickson has benefited from the guidance of his group's older members. Not only have they encouraged him to stay in school, they are determined to help him afford university. Between these two groups, there's a shared commitment to winning by supporting each other together.

PILLARS

♀ OPPORTUNITY

★ EDUCATION

Retoe Enole Keiwua: chairwoman of Inkatenak, the Winning Group

The women's and men's groups of Melelo are family, friends and neighbors from the same tribal clan.
The groups meet often to discuss the challenges they face in the community and create solutions together.
From left to right: Nemuta Keiwua, Meliyo Keiwua, Andrew Tilal Keiwua, Noorkishuru Keiwua,
Beatrice Keiwua, Sinjura Jackson Keiwua, Napolos Keiwua, Nkoje Keiwua, Parsimei Robert Keiwua,
Kilokunye Keiwua, Kitika Keiwua, Nashiru Keiwua, Alex Parmalai Keiwua, Retoe Enole Keiwua (chairwoman),
Peniki Keiwua (chairman), Kitiringa Keiwua, Maleyo Keiwua, Nareiyo Keiwua, Dickson Keiwua
and Nailepu Enole Keiwua.

TOP: *It's especially important for women to come together, "because we are the ones who see the challenges," says chairwoman Retoe Enole Keiwua.*
ABOVE: *Every year, each group holds an election to vote in new leaders. Retoe Enole Keiwua (second from left) is the 2019 chair of the women's group and Peniki Keiwua (far right) is chair of the youth group.*
FACING PAGE: *Clockwise from top left: Nailepu Enole Keiwua, Senchura Jackson Keiwua, Nkonje Keiwua, Maleyo Keiwua, Beatrice Keiwua, Alex Parmalai Keiwua, Nashuru Keiwua, Meliyo Keiwua, Noorkishuru Keiwua and Kilokunye Keiwua.*
FACING PAGE, CENTER: *Nailepu Enole Keiwua, a women's group member, encouraged her son Dickson to join the men's youth group. With financial backing from each of their groups, they're confident Dickson will be able to graduate from high school and go on to college.*

Judy's journey to becoming a ME to WE artisan

A steady job and the promise of a paycheck disrupted the everyday to unlock a future this mama had always hoped for. Meet one of the first women to agree to on-the-job artisan training.

When Judy Cheborkei showed up for her new job, her résumé was made up of farming and firewood-hawking, hustle and hard work. She'd never beaded a single strand of jewelry in her life. But through learning to bead she saw a different future for herself and her family and a chance to realize a belief she'd long suppressed—that she was meant for more.

Sitting in an open field near her children's school in Enelerai, Judy tentatively unwound a piece of clear plastic string, then snipped it to what looked like bracelet length before threading it through a needle. Judy's instructor, a Maasai woman born into a family of beaders, demonstrated how to move the needle in a single swoop to pick up multiple rainbow-hued beads from a tray. Slowly, clumsily, Judy mimicked her movements. So did her new colleagues, long-time Kipsigis friends and neighbors, all beading for the first time, all working for ME to WE Artisans—a decision they hoped would change their futures.

They met for weekly training. At first Judy asked how to do the beading—"Do I pick one bead at a time? Or do I mix? How long should one strand be?"—but every week, she got faster. "I could see the progress. And I loved it, that's why I kept doing it. I enjoyed it, meeting weekly with the other women like that."

Pursuing this new opportunity meant risks for Judy and her family. The time she spent attending the ME to WE Artisans training was precious—time away from tending her corn field, fetching water or collecting firewood to sell at the market. How Judy chose to spend her time determined whether her children had enough food, water and money for school fees. But the mother of five no longer wanted to be defined by her circumstances and was determined to escape the cycle of poverty that had stunted the potential of generations of women in her family.

This wasn't the first time she was trying to break free, but she hoped it would be the last.

PILLARS

 OPPORTUNITY

 EDUCATION

Judy Cheborkei: early adopter, artisan, change-maker

Working to break through

Judy grew up near a town called Mulot, a bustling trading center off the one-lane highway in Narok County, Kenya. Her parents were corn farmers. They owned a small plot of land and also worked for hire on neighboring farms to provide for Judy and her 10 siblings. Her mom foraged and sold firewood, while her dad tended their five cows and planted hay to sell for fodder. Neither of Judy's parents had any formal schooling. They hoped education would open up opportunities for their children.

By the time Judy was in Grade 2, she was helping collect water to wash dishes and clothes. By Grade 5 she was spending weekends working on the farm, planting or weeding, depending on the season. Even at that young age, Judy saw that getting an education could be her ticket to a different life. Her role model was a neighboring doctor with an active practice and a nicer house. Judy wanted to go to college to become a doctor, too.

But in Grade 7 Judy dropped out of school. In the weeks leading up to what would be her last day, she was frequently sent home by her teacher because her parents failed to pay the mandatory fees. "I saw for myself that my parents didn't have money," Judy recalls. One morning, she simply stopped going. She accepted it, and her parents never urged her back.

The teenager began working full-time on the farm, as well as collecting firewood to sell at the market. The money she earned helped pay for the education of her younger siblings. Going to college, let alone finishing high school, was a dead dream. She looked for another goal that she hoped would change her future.

The day Judy was married, she was full of anticipation as she traveled to her new home with her husband. She quickly realized her new house was like her parents': one room, with a small-acreage farm.

"Growing up, I wanted to build a nice house and have chairs and a cupboard and a table. I wanted to buy a cow and a goat, and sheep. And I wanted to have land as well." Those things would have to wait.

With babies came the need for additional income. Judy collected firewood and charcoal, like she'd done with her mom. She'd sell it in Mulot twice a week. The work was long and laborious, but Judy's determination to provide remained steadfast. When her own children were sent home for lack of school fees, Judy feared that her daughters' lives would be no different than her own.

The cycle of poverty looked likely to repeat itself, until a new opportunity disrupted her day-to-day.

ABOVE: *Judy finds a moment for playtime in the morning.*

RIGHT: *Judy waves her children off to school as she prepares for a day working at the Women's Empowerment Centre close to her home in Enelerai.*

The mother of five no longer wanted to be defined by her circumstances and was determined to escape the cycle of poverty that had stunted the potential of generations of women in her family.

Beading is a tradition in Maasai culture. Expert beaders share their knowledge and skill with Kipsigis women eager for the opportunity to earn a fair wage.

For all the ways Judy's life has changed with the security of a steady job, her biggest joy is knowing she can afford her children's education.

A new normal

In 2010, Judy heard about a community meeting to be held at the Motony Primary School, where WE Charity was actively building new classrooms and a water project. Women from surrounding communities were invited. Judy recalls that WE Charity had also started building new classrooms at her children's school in Enelerai, but she wasn't familiar with the organization's other development work.

She was one of more than 200 women to attend the meeting. "Neighbors from all sides came to Motony," Judy remembers. Women from Salabwek, Pimbiniet, Kipsongol and, of course, Enelerai.

The women who had traveled the greatest distance, more than five hours by car, were from an area called Kajiado. They were from the Maasai tribe, and beading is part of their culture, whereas most of the local women in attendance were Kipsigis and had never beaded before.

Sitting on the ground outside the school (there were too many women to fit inside a classroom), the women listened to Leah Lato Toyianka, a Maasai leader from Kajiado. She explained that the women from her community worked with ME to WE, the social enterprise and sister organization to WE Charity, to sell their Maasai jewelry. They earned a steady income, where previously they had struggled to sell their pieces at a local market for a fair price. Mama Leah offered to teach the women gathered how to bead, so they could earn an income as artisans as well.

Judy knew many of the women at the meeting from their long walks together to the market to sell firewood. She and her neighbors eagerly accepted the proposition. "I was very grateful," Judy says. "I was told I would be paid for my work. I never had any doubts that I wanted to do it." This was the opportunity she had been waiting for.

Before long, the training turned into a full-time job. Judy's daily routine shifted. She stopped going for firewood and concentrated her efforts on being the best artisan. Soon, she and the other emerging artisans were making more money than ever before.

With her first pay packet Judy bought the materials to build a toilet for her house. Then she bought a goat, and next, a cow. She outfitted her house with the furniture she had dreamed of growing up—two wooden benches, four chairs, two tables. Soft lace covers were placed over most surfaces, a small style luxury. She and her husband bought more land. She opened a small shop. She also attended financial training provided by WE Charity to manage this influx of new income and started to put away money for savings.

For all the ways Judy's life has changed with the security of a steady job, her biggest joy has been knowing she can afford her children's education. She expects that all her children will surpass her Grade 7 education, hopefully complete high school, maybe attend college.

"I never thought I would get here," Judy says with pride. "My children will be able to get jobs because they'll have an education. Doctors, pilots or even teachers."

In 2018, Judy started to work out of the newly opened Women's Empowerment Centre, a bright building across the road from the school her children attend, with those same neighbors—artisan originals—who were present at the initial training. ME to WE Artisans employs more than 1,600 women in Kenya. Although many women choose to work from home, every day more than a hundred women arrive at the center (their office) ready for work.

As always, Judy will be there, deftly tying a knot in the thin thread, pulling tightly so the beads kiss one another, completing her piece before she expertly moves on to the next one. Whether she makes a staple ME to WE Rafiki friendship chain or a unique item for a seasonal collection, her creation goes beyond the individual piece. She creates *kimnatet*—the Kipsigis word for empowerment.

WANDA O'BRIEN

FACING PAGE TOP: *The Women's Empowerment Centre acts as headquarters for ME to WE Artisans in Kenya, but it also offers financial literacy training, banking facilities and childcare services for working moms.*
FACING PAGE BOTTOM: *Evelyne Rop, ME to WE Artisans coordinator, reviews the quantity of beads needed for the latest order.*
ABOVE: *Nashilu Dapash (left) and Judy (right) bead Rafikis, friendship chains made by ME to WE Artisans and worn around the world.*

Each morning, Judy prepares tea for her children. Once they are at school, she splits her time between working at the Women's Empowerment Centre and managing the small shop she's opened with her artisan earnings.

A center of their own

PILLAR: OPPORTUNITY

At the Women's Empowerment Centre in rural Narok County, the rustle of beads signals the start of the workday. Artisans settle in at wooden tables and arrange their few supplies: a needle, a spool of thread, a bowl full of glass beads in bold or pastel shades, depending on the project ahead. For the women who gather here each day, transforming traditional crafts into a healthy income, the center is more than a makers' studio. It's the site of new beginnings.

When WE Charity first partnered with communities in Narok, they worked together to identify existing strengths that could be leveraged to raise family incomes. Within the Maasai community, beadwork was a rich cultural legacy, a skill passed down through generations and an untapped opportunity. ME to WE, a social enterprise and WE Charity's sister organization, launched ME to WE Artisans, a program that sought to connect talented women to an international market for their products and secure them a fair wage in return.

The first artisans employed by ME to WE beaded from home, weaving the new job into their daily routines. They started with single-strand bracelets called Rafikis—Swahili for "friend"—to honor the nascent connections with supporters around the world. As demand for these products grew, ME to WE Artisans needed a coordinating center to manage large orders. In 2014, the women set up shop in a borrowed community hall in the village of Enelerai, sharing a compound with the local primary school. Women from Maasai and Kipsigis communities—tribes that had historically been at odds—found themselves working side by side toward common goals: sending their children to school, maintaining their health, accessing nutritious food and clean water, and saving for the future. Old rivalries gave way to friendly competition and a deep sense of camaraderie and cohesion. ME to WE called the space the Women's Empowerment Centre.

Building on the success of this venture, WE opened a new Women's Empowerment Centre in 2018, a cluster of bright red-roofed buildings adjacent to Baraka Hospital and the WE College. The center is not simply housing for ME to WE Artisans production and supplies, it's also a hub where community members can access WE Charity's Opportunity Pillar programming.

With a classroom and a computer lab, the center provides financial literacy workshops and training on other income-generating skills. It also features a banking hall where the women can undertake secure financial transactions and increase their financial management skills. An onsite daycare gives mothers a safe place to leave their children while they bead or use the center's programs and services.

Every element of the Women's Empowerment Centre reflects the insight and input of the women who gather here. They have helped to build it from the ground up, and rightly feel pride and ownership over the space. In the years to come, they will continue to shape it into what they need it to be—a place to unearth capabilities and elaborate designs or to recall the simple friendship bracelets that started it all, one bead following another.

Infrastructure in Kenya

Beneath the inspirational stories of transformation in Kenya's Narok and Bomet Counties that this book celebrates are the bricks and mortar that form the literal foundations upon which so much of WE Charity's work is built: from primary schools to award-winning high schools to a rural college, a hospital and health center, water stations, and so much more.

WE Charity supporters not only fund transformative programs that help families to create their own solutions to end poverty, they also come together to finance the construction of significant infrastructure projects.

Kisaruni Group of Schools administration block

The First Lady of Kenya, Margaret Kenyatta, visits WE College with Craig Kielburger.

The path that leads into Laila Primary School

New primary schoolrooms in Rongena

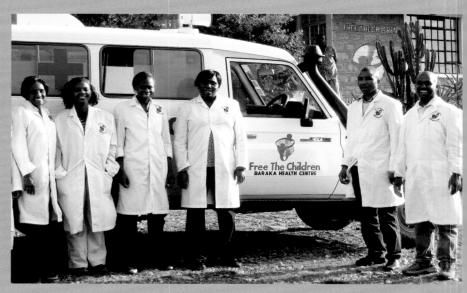

The Baraka health team with the ambulance used for mobile clinics. Bringing essential equipment and medicine to remote communities has remained a staple part of the hospital's mandate.

The water tower in Oloirien community

Be the change

Kisaruni high school students improve their computer skills in the technology lab.

Kishon Health Centre provides services that complement Baraka Hospital, including specialized services in dialysis and optometry.

Solar panels provide electricity to run community water projects.

Local residents access clean water through community-run kiosks.

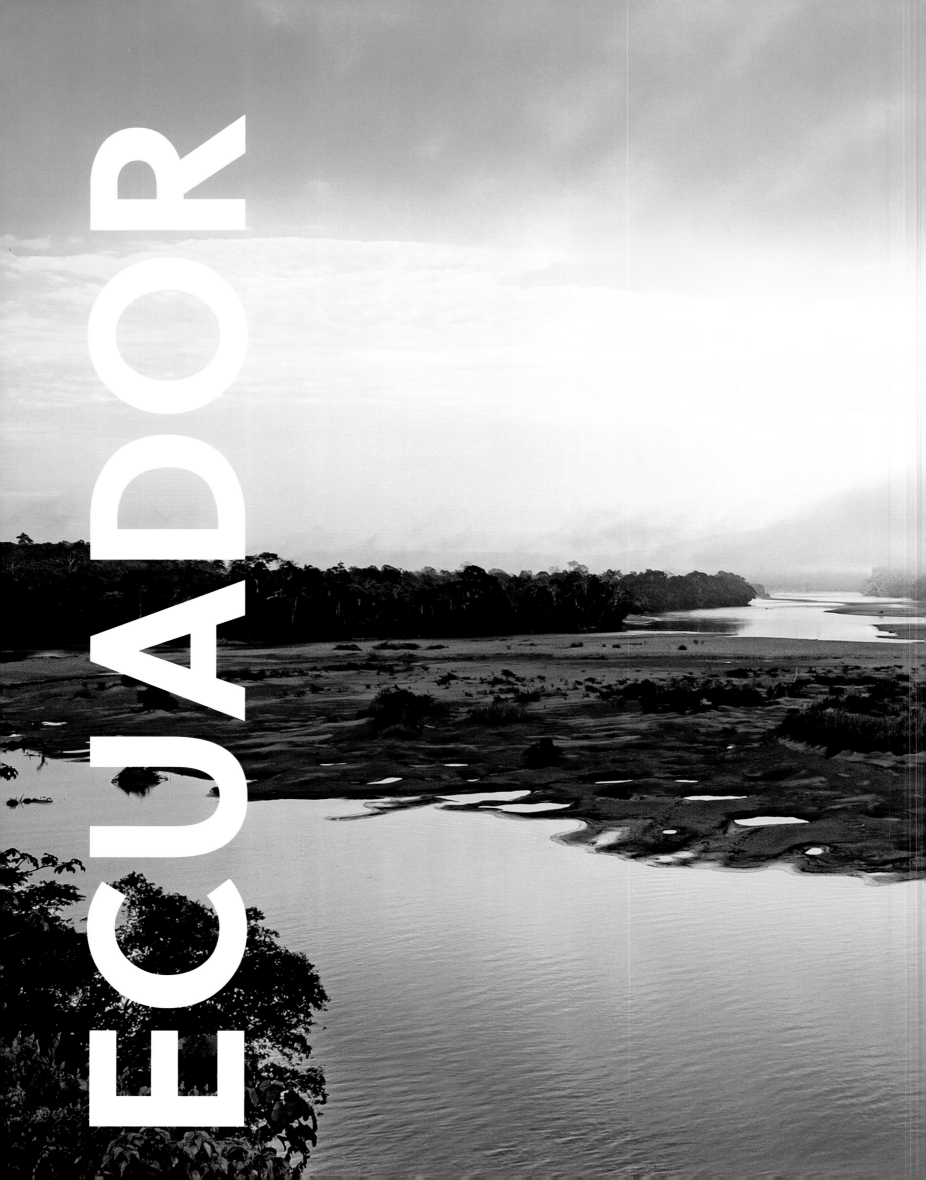

ECUADOR

Trouble on the mountain and the marvelous *minga*

"In Ecuador's highlands we discovered a philosophy that changed the trajectory of our charity and reordered our lives."

BY MARC KIELBURGER, CO-FOUNDER OF WE

Craig and I were still teenagers when we witnessed something unexpected in the mountains of Ecuador that will stay with us for life. It reaffirmed our belief in the inherent goodness of people and introduced us to a philosophy that would define the WE movement. Let me tell you about a *minga*.

It was March of 1999 and we were traveling by pack mule to build a schoolroom in Cruz del Arenal, at the base of Mount Chimborazo, more than 13,000 feet above sea level. We were leading a group of student volunteers on their spring break, and we had two weeks to complete the job before our flight home to Canada. But obstacles presented themselves from the get-go. Although our team made it up to the village, our building supplies did not. Harvest season had caused a high-altitude traffic jam, the agrarian version of rush hour. Mules loaded with produce filled the steep switchbacks that led to markets in the valley. Our lumber and cement, on its way up, had to wait days for the mule convoys to pass. We were preparing for the worst, a months-long delay until the next group of volunteers could arrive to complete the job. Even when the materials finally arrived at the build site, we felt we had let down the community that had trusted us with this important task.

We sought out the village chief, an elderly woman who listened stoically as a translator explained our predicament. We had to tell her we were in danger of delaying the project. There was a tense pause before she responded, "No problem," matter-of-factly. And then: "I'll call a minga." She walked outside and, with a voice that shook the birds from their trees, announced to the village: "Tomorrow there will be a minga!"

A minga? Our interpreter wasn't sure of the word's English equivalent. He was translating from the Indigenous Kichwa. Whatever the word meant, the chief seemed completely calm, happy even. We wondered if we'd explained ourselves properly. This was not the reaction of a woman who understood that we'd leave her with a construction site instead of a schoolroom.

We tried our best to work late into the night, but as it got dark, we hit our thumbs more than the nails and eventually went to bed. After a restless night, we woke early and were surprised to find more than a hundred people gathered in the village square: farmers armed with hand tools and women with babies strapped to their backs. There were old men and young boys with energy to burn. Children had been sent to neighboring villages to spread the word, and people had converged from miles around. Ready with equipment, they were there to help build, though some lived too far away to ever send their own children to the school.

We had estimated that the construction project would take another full week to complete, but we finished that same afternoon. Trusses were built, bricks were laid. Everything from the rebar to the roof was installed. We celebrated that evening with a feast. Our team was ecstatic, if still confused about how it had all come together. We approached the village chief to find out more about mingas. Through our translator, she explained the concept: a minga is a call to action for the betterment of all. She went on to explain that in North America, people often think, "We are a community, so we must help each other." But for the Puruhá Indians, as they refer to themselves, it is through helping others that they become a community. All the country's Indigenous tribes, and many non-Indigenous Ecuadorians, adhere to this philosophy. A minga is people coming together for the common good. It is the strength of all of us—of *we*.

When the chief asked us about the English equivalent for *minga*, we were stumped. It's not exactly volunteering, which can be done alone. "Barn raising" is a phrase, sure, but I've never seen an actual barn raising in my lifetime. We couldn't find the word in our own culture.

In 2013, WE Charity expanded its presence in Ecuador to Napo province in the Amazon basin. The charity traces its roots in the country back to the minga tradition, a local philosophy that rallies communities for the common good. Today people still come together in a minga to build a school or dig a well.

Cultural imports

We thought we should import a bit of that community-first mindset. In North America, where individuality rules, happiness is equated with wealth accumulation, even if this pursuit often leaves people isolated and unfulfilled. Through international development work in rural communities, I've met people who value above all else their deep connections to family and neighbors. All of us on that Ecuador trip wanted to bring home that perspective to share with others.

The minga philosophy reordered our lives and inspired us to write a new book, *Me to We: Finding Meaning in a Material World*. Craig and I decided that we wanted not only to work with communities overseas but also to forge deeper connections to our communities at home. So we called our own minga, and we named it WE Day. This youth empowerment event, held in cities around the world, was built on the minga philosophy. It started with a few thousand students in Toronto, but over the years, more than one million students have attended WE Day events around the world, earning their tickets through service to their local or global communities. Youth engaged in our WE Schools service-learning program have logged tens of millions of volunteer hours and raised millions of dollars for local and global causes. All of this grew out of the minga philosophy, as did the social enterprise that Craig and I founded, called ME to WE, after our book. We launched this social enterprise because we wanted to help consumers consider their spending habits and turn daily choices into a force for good in the world.

Craig Kielburger visits Ecuador's Chimborazo province, one of two regions in the country where WE Charity operates. Local children benefit from the organization's educational programming, which increases access to primary education in the remote mountainous region.

Our current development work in Ecuador is deeply connected to that fateful trip in 1999. Mingas are still an essential part of every construction project, planned at regular meetings between community leaders and WE Charity's country team. During builds, there are designated "minga days" that bring together our staff, volunteers and local community members to work side by side, dig foundations or raise a water tower. This initial engagement and buy-in also ensures community commitment to maintain and grow projects over the long term, once WE Charity completes our work in a village. It's a great sacrifice for farmers to leave their fields and livestock, but their desire to advance their individual goals is outweighed by their resolve to help the community.

Rural Ecuador has a history of exploitation that began with Spanish colonization and carried on through the hacienda system, with parcels of land divided unjustly according to a rigid hierarchy. People on the land were subject to the rule of elite hacienda owners, most of whom were left in power when the Spanish departed. Hacienda land dwellers had to provide free labor to landowners. The crops they grew became the landowner's property. Their personal freedoms were also denied; they needed permission even to marry. This system persisted until agricultural reform in the 1960s, but the hacienda legacy is still evident in the distribution of resources, education levels and access to opportunities for Indigenous peoples. Newly granted land access did not erase hundreds of years of oppression.

In the province of Chimborazo, where I witnessed my first minga, 40 percent of the population are Indigenous peoples, and 90 percent of children live in poverty. Remote and sparsely populated villages are cut off from basic resources, including access to primary education and other vital infrastructure. In 2006, WE Charity launched our five-pillar development model in Chimborazo, going beyond school building to include water and sanitation projects, health care and economic empowerment, as well as agriculture and food security programs. Local children now have access to quality primary education, which includes instruction in their first language, Kichwa. These projects help to raise the rate of primary school completion while preserving Indigenous cultural heritage.

In 2013, WE Charity expanded our work to Napo province in Ecuador's Amazon region, where we partnered with riverside communities to implement all five pillars of our development model. Among our many projects, we designed one of the region's most advanced water treatment systems, installed in the community of Los Rios. Although the Amazon rainforest is one of the wettest places on the planet, pollution and climate change have made access to clean water a challenge. But the treatment system pipes clean water into every home in the village, including that of the Ramos family, whose story you will find in this section. Rosa Ramos is 98, one of five generations living in Los Rios. Her family previously had no option but to drink river water, risking illness with every sip.

Health care is also a challenge in this region. Most villages along the Napo River are accessible only via canoe. The local health clinic once operated from a boat that traveled up and down the river, but it sunk years ago and the wreck became a relic, a taunting reminder of the fragility of life. When a new clinic was finally constructed on land, it was ravaged by termites and unrelenting rain. Rather than risk a visit to this compromised structure, locals opted to deal with health issues on their own.

WE Charity rebuilt the clinic in 2016. Quality infrastructure renewed confidence in its services, and health metrics steadily improved. Mobile clinics now travel to the farthest reaches of the jungle, where a dentist and a general practitioner set up temporary exam rooms in local schools for students who can't make it to the permanent clinic for checkups.

In both Napo and Chimborazo, we work with historically marginalized Indigenous communities where employment opportunities are scarce. Girls especially tend to cut their studies short and so have fewer prospects. Teen marriage and low family incomes mean the dropout rate for girls is high.

San Miguel was the site of WE Charity's first high school in Ecuador, but getting girls to class proved difficult. The teenage girls of this Andean village were shy and withdrawn, having grown up with their own wants and needs subordinated to those of male relatives. Once married, they were expected to serve their husbands. Life is harder for girls in most parts of the world, but in rural Ecuador, *machismo*, or male dominance, is an accepted cultural norm.

The girls needed a stepping stone to find the confidence to enroll in school. WE Charity started the first girls' club in San Miguel in 2010, where young women age 15 and up could learn leadership skills while earning an income to help fund their education. In this section, you'll meet Lucia Yasaca Daquilema, who at age 13 overcame her paralyzing fear of public speaking to declare her desire to join this club of older girls. She and the group now turn traditional weaving techniques into contemporary accessories that they can sell. They also raise and sell guinea pigs, a vital and popular source of protein. The girls' club is a space for young women to establish self-confidence and independence, and to earn the money they need to stay in school.

Women's groups in our partner communities began to cultivate similar opportunities. They officially joined ME to WE's Artisans program in 2015, creating handcrafted jewelry, woven alpaca blankets and other accessories for an international market. The ME to WE Artisans program honors Indigenous cultures, providing women with the resources to turn time-honored traditions into business opportunities and economic empowerment. WE Charity takes the same approach in our work with Ecuadorian famers, providing training to help them turn conventional crops into sustainable livelihoods.

In Napo province, cacao cultivation is common, but many farmers lack knowledge of best practices in irrigation, pruning and planting. Cacao is a finicky crop that requires years of maintenance before the first harvest; so many fields are left abandoned when trees fail to yield fruit. In 2019, the WE Agricultural Learning Center (ALC) held its inaugural training session for farmers in the Napo region. Demand for training was so high that the workshop was moved to a larger location to accommodate the crowd. Though WE Charity had previously provided training to local farmers, the ALC formalized instruction and allowed for practice in our demonstration field, a 170-acre plot that sustainably produces food for the surrounding

In 2013, WE Charity expanded its presence in Ecuador to Napo province in the Amazon basin, where many local farmers grow cacao, a difficult crop to care for. Melquiades Coello is head instructor at WE's Agricultural Learning Center (ALC), where local farmers learn about soil composition in the classroom and perfect their trimming techniques in the training field. The ALC is designed to improve farmers' fields, incomes and future prospects.

communities, as well as for travelers visiting WE Charity projects in Ecuador. This once barren land is now flourishing with crops nurtured by our farmers in training, who see their new knowledge of tools and techniques as indispensable. Ongoing training in eco-conscious agriculture will improve cacao cash crop yields and nourish families in the region.

ME to WE Chocolate launched in 2017, selling Fair Trade–certified bars made with cacao beans grown in Ecuador, its partial proceeds supporting farmers and their families. It's a closed-loop system that provides employment as well as funding for community development projects—such as classrooms for the farmers' children. For a culture that values community progress over individual gain, the closed-loop system is a perfect fit. Participating farmers produce more crops and improve their families' lives, but their efforts also fund village development projects and boost the local economy. That isn't charity; that's a community rallying for change. That's a minga.

Impact at a glance

Focus on Chimborazo

Population: 458,581
Languages: Spanish is the official language; Kichwa is the most commonly spoken Indigenous language and is predominant where WE Charity works.
Population below poverty line: 44%
Children under five affected by stunting: 49%
Agriculture as income: 33%
Access to clean water: 42%

Focus on Napo

Population: 103,697
Population below poverty line: 39%
Children under 5 affected by stunting: 28%
Agriculture as income: 90%
Access to clean water: 59%

*The above statistics are drawn from Ecuadorian government reports

Chimborazo province is in the highlands of Ecuador, amidst the Andean mountain range. It has one of the largest Indigenous populations in the country. These groups were subject to discrimination through the hacienda system, a land estate scheme established under colonial rule that stripped Indigenous populations of their rights. Although Ecuador has a high national literacy rate, illiteracy is common in Kichwa communities because of a lack of educational opportunities. Limited job options, unproductive land and disputed access to water resources continue to trap communities in poverty. WE Charity works in solidarity with rural communities by building on traditional strengths and knowledge and improving access to vital resources.

WE Charity expanded its Ecuador programming to the Amazon basin in 2013, partnering with Indigenous populations living along the Napo River. Napo province is home to the Amazon rainforest, the largest tropical rainforest in the world. The lush jungle conceals the challenges faced by local residents in accessing basic resources, including education, clean water, health care, nutritious food and income opportunities. This region is home to thousands of Indigenous people who have lived there for millennia and are among the most vulnerable in Latin America because of their limited authority over agricultural land use, labor opportunities (particularly for women) and health care.

Impact by the numbers by 2020

☆ EDUCATION
100+ schoolrooms built, including classrooms, teacher offices and libraries

◍ WATER
7 water systems built or rehabilitated to provide clean water to students and families

♥ HEALTH
1,500+ people from 12 communities accessing health services through Mondaña Health Center

800+ patients served by 34+ mobile clinics reaching 15 remote communities

◍ FOOD
170+ acres in WE's Agricultural Learning Center, opened in 2018 to provide training to farmers

♀ OPPORTUNITY
82,000+ pieces created by Ecuador artisans, driving a sustainable source of income for their families

A traveling dad finds his way home

Carlitos Daquilema's hands reveal the marks of a maker. His hardened calluses stretch over rough palms to document decades of labor. He is a builder and a father, and through an opportunity with WE Charity, he found a way to be best at both.

Carlitos Daquilema stood at a crossroads most mornings, waiting with a shovel.

Like many migrant workers, Carlitos would leave his wife and children in their rural village in Ecuador's Chimborazo province while he traveled to densely populated urban centers in search of work.

Holding his tool in hand, measuring tape attached to his belt, he'd jockey for position beside other men along the roadside of a busy intersection in cities such as Cuenca or Riobamba, nestled between the Andes Mountains. Together, the men waited for a drive-by job offer.

Carlitos had known this wandering life since he was eight, spending summers shadowing his father, moving from worksite to distant worksite to earn his own money to buy pencils and books for the upcoming school year, all the while imagining becoming an architect or engineer. But after primary school, at age 12, Carlitos was forced to drop out. There was no high school in his small community of San Miguel and the costs to travel to a school elsewhere were impossible for his family to cover. So the construction site became his classroom, and his dad, the teacher.

Carlitos stopped dreaming of professions that required higher learning, and instead followed in his father's footsteps to find work as a builder on residential or commercial job sites. Sometimes he'd get picked up early by a crew and was paid in cash. Those were the good days. On the so-so days, Carlitos would put in a full day's work but receive only a portion of the promised payment. On bad days, he would wait for hours until the sun dipped low in the sky and then go back to a rented room with empty pockets, steeling himself to return to the intersection the following day.

Back home, Carlitos was also building a family. He and his wife, Rosario, started to have children, and his earnings became even more important. Once he'd made enough money to provide for his family for one or two months, Carlitos boarded a public bus for the journey back to San Miguel, back to the isolated cluster of households in the Palmira Desert, and the poor soil and few job prospects that kept men away.

PILLAR

★ EDUCATION

Carlitos Daquilema: father, builder, provider

ABOVE: *Rosario Daquilema with her daughter Maria Delfina, her fourth child and the first person in the family to graduate high school.*
FACING PAGE: *Carlitos in his role as WE Charity foreman on a construction site in the Amazon*

Carlitos was on a rare visit home in 2008 when WE Charity held an inaugural community meeting in San Miguel to discuss the future of education for local children. The existing primary school, the one Carlitos had attended as a boy and the one his own children now attended, was too small, and there was still no high school. He went to the meeting determined that his children would have options that weren't available to him growing up.

In Ecuador's rural communities like San Miguel, limited educational opportunities and intergenerational poverty are unwelcome legacies of the hacienda system. This land estate scheme started under colonial rule in the 1530s and continued until the 1960s. It exploited Indigenous populations, stripping families like Carlitos' of their land and rights. Although no longer practiced, the system left rural Indigenous communities lacking access to clean water, health resources, viable land for crops, job opportunities and quality education.

In 2006, WE Charity began partnering with Indigenous communities in the Andes mountain range to help restore those rights and break generational cycles of poverty, by implementing its five-pillar approach to sustainable development. In partnership with the local government and community leaders, WE Charity designed a school campus for San Miguel that would not only add new classrooms to the primary school but would also include a brand-new government-funded high school.

Carlitos' youngest children had a real chance at a secondary school education, provided he and the fathers and mothers of San Miguel picked up their tools and put their hard-won construction skills to work on the most significant project every built in their community. There is a long-standing tradition in Ecuador of people readily volunteering their time to work for the common good of everyone. While there is no equivalent word for it in English, in Kichwa (the most common Indigenous language in Ecuador), this practice of coming together is called a *minga*.

Several mingas were called. The first minga was to build the fence that would surround the future campus. Carlitos reorganized his travel to be at home. At least one representative from each of the 260 families living in San Miguel participated. Rosario joined her husband, putting her own hands to use in the construction. The mother of seven didn't want her children to repeat her life of illiteracy.

Carlitos' commitment, passion and experience stood out. WE Charity hired him as head foreman to lead the construction work and manage the mingas. This career shift ended his relentless search for work, Carlitos explains in a mixture of Spanish and Kichwa. "I no longer needed to go look in the city for a room, or find a friend, or beg someone to lend me a small room. I became more confident and hopeful."

During construction, Carlitos pored over the architect's designs and learned to read blueprints. His desire to become a construction expert was reawakened as he cut his teeth on a more complicated floor plan. The high school would be the first two-story building in the community. As WE Charity installed clean water stations at the school and built new and better latrines, a playground, a kitchen and a school garden, Carlitos was involved at every step, gaining experience and a sense of job security.

Carlitos became emotional when he thought about his journey with WE Charity. The quiet man who smiles easily now had tears in his eyes. "I remember when I finished the first set of classrooms, my daughter came home with her backpack, and she said, 'Dad, how did it happen?' And I said, 'It is for you. You have to take advantage of it.'"

Carlitos passes on his construction knowledge to his son Luis Ruben, who wants to become an electrician. Before that, he plans to be the first male in the family to graduate high school.

There is a long-standing tradition in Ecuador of people readily volunteering their time to work for the common good of everyone. ... this practice of coming together is called a **minga***.*

FACING PAGE: *Rosario participated in mingas alongside her husband, Carlitos, to help build the school for their children. She's also a farmer and raises guinea pigs, a high-protein staple in the region's diet.*

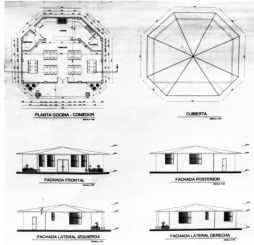

TOP: *San Miguel school campus welcomes primary and high school students.*
ABOVE: *The architect's design for a school kitchen. Carlitos keenly pores over the blueprints, thirsty to enhance his knowledge.*

On the road again

With construction underway in San Miguel, WE Charity continued its work with other Indigenous communities throughout Chimborazo. Carlitos became the go-to construction foreman and ambassador for WE Charity, on a mission to improve access to education for more would-be students. He motivated parents to volunteer in mingas by sharing the success story of San Miguel's school and worked side by side with the architect, who joked that Carlitos was going to put him out of a job. Carlitos wasn't just reading blueprints, he was helping to create them.

When WE Charity expanded to Napo province in 2013 to partner with Indigenous and rural communities living in the Amazon rainforest, Carlitos was once again away from home. This time, he wasn't leaving to find work—he was leaving *because of* his work. He loaded his tools into a canoe and traveled to communities dotting the Napo River to lead school infrastructure projects.

As Carlitos built new schools, he also rebuilt himself into the role model he had always wanted to be for his children.

The San Miguel school campus was the largest project undertaken in the community. Through the partnership with WE Charity, students in the community access primary and secondary education. Parents send their children to school with confidence that they can attain a high school diploma.

"Before, I could not be in peace, but thank God I started with WE," he shares. "I remember when I was a boy studying in my classroom and it was only a block house with a thatched roof. I always remember that when I see my children. Now they are in a nice classroom, studying year after year, and they are moving forward. That's a joy."

In 2015, the first cohort graduated from San Miguel High School. Years of labor and commitment were realized as young men and women became the first in their families to earn a diploma and start a new community tradition—high school graduation—that would continue year after year.

WANDA O'BRIEN

The construction site in the Los Rios community is in the Amazon rainforest. As WE Charity's head foreman, Carlitos travels to WE Charity project sites across Ecuador to lead construction crews and organize mingas. In Los Rios, the team builds the school kitchen, new classrooms and a clean water system.

During mingas, moms and dads dedicate their time and expertise. Los Rios community president Juan Granja (above, far left), is a WE Charity advocate who believes education is the cornerstone of prosperity. "The school is a luxury for the community. With the new classrooms, the students will listen to the teachers easier and will concentrate more. They will have the desire to study."

Right of passage: attending high school is no longer a distant dream

PILLAR: EDUCATION

For young people coming of age in rural and remote parts of Ecuador—whether in the arid valley of San Miguel or the Andes rooftop in Shuid in Chimborazo province—the toughest part of high school isn't gossip or peer pressure; it's just getting yourself to the front door.

In the Chimborazo highlands, home to the largest number of Indigenous communities in Ecuador, WE Charity has been working since 1999 to help clear the path to education and opportunity.

High school students in San Miguel used to start their day with an hour-and-a-half-long trek across a desert landscape, then a ride on the public bus to the nearest town. Very few students had the stamina to endure the two-way journey on a daily basis.

For youth in the mountaintop village of Shuid, at an altitude of more than 12,000 feet, walking wasn't even an option. The closest secondary school was a 30-minute ride away, but only a hired van would make the treacherous descent through the clouds, and securing a seat cost a family 25 percent of their monthly income. Parents fortunate enough to consider this option could send only one child, and only ever a boy. For most, however, the expense was out of the question.

When going to high school was the exception rather than the rule, it was common for girls to prepare for early marriage, while young men migrated to the city in search of work as laborers. For those left behind, the lack of prospects fueled teen pregnancy and a high rate of alcohol abuse.

In 2008 and 2009, WE Charity's community partnerships grew to include both San Miguel and Shuid; education programming focused first on primary education and then worked to tackle the barriers to high school, by allowing students to study in their own communities. San Miguel's secondary school opened its doors in 2013, and Shuid's followed in 2017, radically changing the landscape of opportunities for young people. San Miguel's first batch of high school graduates landed jobs with government-run nurseries and seniors' homes, while others have found positions in the cities or gone on to university. And in Shuid, the community is watching to see what the first graduating class will go on to do with their diplomas in hand.

WE Charity built the high school in Shuid, a community in the Andes Mountains often cloaked in clouds, giving young people access to post-secondary education.

TOP AND ABOVE: *In high school, students are introduced to new subjects, including statistics, entrepreneurship and English.*
LEFT: *Shuid's inaugural graduation ceremony, in July 2019*
FOLLOWING SPREAD: *The mountains used to limit a student's access to school. With primary and secondary schools established within a community, the sweeping mountain range is no longer an obstacle to education.*

After WE Charity finished construction, local leaders continued to organize mingas to make improvements to the school campus. Maria Francisca Malan (top left) carries bricks to reinforce the retaining wall surrounding the campus where her children study, reinforcing the notion that education is here to stay.

Ines Hurtado, Lucia Guaman and Carmen Sanay volunteer their time for their children's school.

No boys allowed

Girls' clubs are giving teens in rural Ecuador the tools they need to continue their studies and tap into sisterly solidarity. This is girl power.

Lucia Yasaca Daquilema held the brown-spotted guinea pig for the first time, feeling its weight and warmth. She had gone through months of training for this very moment, but now doubt was creeping up. How could she, a timid 15-year-old girl without any prior experience, take care of this furry creature whose heartbeat pulsed against her palms? It seemed like her whole future depended on the rodent.

If she and the 14 other girls' club members not only kept these guinea pigs alive but also successfully bred them, they could earn enough money to finance their studies. For Lucia, this was an opportunity to be the first girl in her family to complete high school. Her three elder sisters had been married as teens because her family couldn't afford the cost of school. Their potential had gone untapped and they came to rely on their husbands. Lucia feared she was headed down the same path.

The guinea pigs were her ticket to a high school diploma. And the girls' club of San Miguel offered the necessary leadership skills and coaching to break the status quo in a hypermasculine culture.

For Maria Angela Pacheco, WE Charity program coordinator and girls' club founder, the link between girls' empowerment and education is personal. She grew up in an Indigenous community in Ecuador's highlands and hustled her way through high school, funded by the homemade crafts her mother sold. After graduating at 18, she defied protocol and ran for president of her community, the first woman who had dared to attempt that. She won, she says, not because the men trusted her, but because they wanted to prove that a woman wouldn't be able to handle the position. They voted her in to watch her fail.

Instead, her time as president cemented her will to foster women's empowerment among the girls and women of Santa Anita de Pulingui, her community in the Andes highlands. "Whenever I led a meeting, I saw women listening attentively, as if they wanted to say something but felt they could not," Maria Angela remembers. The women's self-censorship nagged at her.

PILLARS

★ EDUCATION
♀ OPPORTUNITY

Lucia Yasaca Daquilema: advocate, entrepreneur, role model

After her presidential term ended, she worked odd jobs to put herself through university and graduated with a degree in local development. Upon graduating, she dedicated herself to women's issues in Indigenous communities in Chimborazo, helping female artisans earn a living independent of their husbands and encouraging those who dreamed of an education to return to school.

In 2009, WE Charity was scouting for a leader to work with teenage girls at risk of dropping out of school. Maria Angela applied for the role because she saw an opportunity to provide girls with mentorship that could change the course of their lives. The first community she visited with WE Charity was Lucia's home of San Miguel. WE Charity was already working with the community to construct its first high school. But as it was, very few girls were finishing primary school. To get them to high school, the community needed more than a building.

Maria Angela called a meeting to pitch a radical idea to parents and teachers: a girls-only extracurricular program—no boys allowed—for students 15 and older. She believed a girls' club would provide insulation against threats to their self-esteem and act as an incubator for their potential. It would teach girls to use their voice in school so they wouldn't be afraid to speak up as grown women. Their mothers were part of that same generation who would silence themselves in Maria Angela's community meetings.

At first there was little interest. Parents were skeptical of allowing their daughters to gather with their female friends, fearful that it was an indulgent waste of time. Besides, once finished with primary school, they said, their daughters should be married. Maria Angela had encountered the same cultural hurdles throughout her own life and realized she needed to help parents see the practical value of an education, and of raising confident young women. She needed an incentive.

At the next meeting in San Miguel, Maria Angela explained that WE Charity would train the girls to raise and sell guinea pigs, a high-protein staple in the region, which would provide additional income to families. The girls would also use their time together to make and sell traditional jewelry, another micro-business. Part-time work for their daughters was enticing for parents, but it came with a condition. In order to be eligible to participate, girls had to attend high school, using the proceeds from their business ventures to support their studies.

Lucia's dad attended both meetings. He thought about his youngest daughter. At 13, Lucia was smart and hard-working, but also shy and cautious, rarely making eye contact. He listened when Maria Angela told him that educating girls means a better standard of living for the whole family.

He approached Maria Angela to ask if an exception could be made for Lucia, who was below the age requirement to join the club. Maria Angela suggested that Lucia give a speech about why she wanted to join the girls-only group, as an opportunity for the teen to start to exercise her own agency.

ABOVE: *Handwoven jewelry and traditional hair pieces called* cintas *are sold locally.*
FACING PAGE: *Lucia was inspired by women's rights advocate Maria Angela Pacheco, the founder of the girls' club program.*

Facing her audience—Maria Angela and the club members—Lucia took a deep breath, just like her dad had told her to, and began to speak. She explained that she knew she would be the youngest member of the club, but promised to work just as hard as the older girls to fight for her education. She told them it was her dream to graduate high school.

Lucia became the youngest founding member. She had seen the value of using her voice.

The girls' club started meeting weekly, three hours after class every Thursday. Maria Angela shared her own story with the members, of how she broke with tradition to make history. "I told them, 'No one can come and take your rights.'"

Together, they learned about women's rights in Ecuador, about leadership skills and business management. They started training with a veterinarian to gear up for the arrival of their guinea pig, which they would receive in the third year of the program.

Lucia got to work, building a guinea pig shelter beside her house. A healthy guinea pig would sell for up to US$10, a significant contribution to her school fund. To start, each member was responsible for ten females and two males. Lucia put her fear aside once again and tentatively brought her herd home.

Maria Angela (back row, center) with the inaugural San Miguel girls' club. Although members have graduated from high school, they continue to be each other's core support system.

The girls took on all aspects of care, keeping the pens clean, collecting food in the fields for feedings, and learning to make official records of sales. They shared their progress at meetings and gained a feeling for business and economics, as well as a confidence boost.

Lucia became a star performer, just as she'd promised in her speech. She meticulously followed the instructions of the veterinarian, slowly increased the population of her herd, and then started selling to people in her community and the surrounding area, often getting the full $10. Soon she had more than 70 guinea pigs.

As the herd grew, so did Lucia. She was in high school, speaking up in class and committed to graduating.

"When I started in the girls' club, everything was difficult for me," Lucia says. "I only went to school, did what the teacher said, and I was afraid of everything. With the help of the club I learned to lose my fear, to be able to speak in public and to ask questions with confidence."

Her newfound confidence would soon be put to the ultimate test.

In her last year of high school, Lucia's family accepted a proposal for her to be married. Everything she had worked so hard to attain went out of focus. Would she be able to graduate? Would her new husband let her continue with her business? Early marriage and teen pregnancy had stopped her sisters' potential. Now her diploma was in jeopardy.

Club members show off their latest creations.

Mustering her courage, Lucia told her parents she didn't want to marry the young man, but instead wanted to finish high school. If she had stayed silent, she doesn't know what would have happened. Both she and Maria Angela think she would have been married and may not have finished school. But she spoke up, and her parents listened. In July 2018, Lucia graduated from San Miguel High School.

The former girls' club members continue to meet regularly, some bringing their babies on their backs. They are both breadwinners and mothers, married but still independent.

Lucia did marry, but only after graduating. Her husband supports her work. She credits her life's diverted path to Maria Angela. "She taught me to say that nothing is impossible, despite being a woman. She taught me to be brave."

Maria Angela shares her pride in Lucia's progress. "Lucia has always been a strong, motivated girl. She is very intelligent. She will use her story to motivate others." Lucia has already encouraged her younger nieces and other girls in the community to stay in school.

Maria Angela, meanwhile, has started more girls' clubs in Chimborazo province, where San Miguel is located, and farther afield, in the Amazon rainforest. But the first club members will always stay with her. "I carry them in my heart," she says. "They are my inspiration."

WANDA O'BRIEN

WE Charity's girls' club helps teenage girls stay in school

PILLARS: EDUCATION AND OPPORTUNITY

In Ecuador's highlands, the formal gathering of girls is a small act of defiance against the status quo. WE Charity, alongside Indigenous women's rights leader Maria Angela Pacheco, launched the first girls' club in Chimborazo in 2010 to support girls at risk of dropping out of school. The program is dedicated to helping teens grow into confident, articulate leaders.

In the rural communities where WE Charity works, a strong patriarchal undercurrent known as *machismo*, or male chauvinism, limits the potential of girls. Girls are much less likely to graduate from primary school than their male peers. The chances of girls continuing to high school are even slimmer, because of strained family finances, early marriage and teen pregnancy. Starting high school is a feat, and graduating is a triumph.

Girls' club members participate in a customized after-school program that pairs personal development and leadership training with income-generating activities to afford high school. The program expanded to the Amazon in 2016, so that across Ecuador girls find solidarity and friendship with an exclusive membership that helps them claim their rights and shape their futures.

FACING PAGE, TOP: *Maria Angela Pacheco (top left) is a WE Charity coordinator and the founder of the girls' club program. Her high school workshops teach teenage girls about women's rights and financial management to unlock their leadership potential.*

ABOVE: *Alicia Guaraca (left) is a role model for her peers. She's a quick learner who shares her knowledge with the other girls, like her friend Rosa Malan (right).*

LEFT: *Members of the Shuid girls' club all hope to graduate high school. From left to right: Jakeline Chafla, Alicia Guaraca, Maria Belen Hurtado, Blanca Sanay, Monica Chafla, Laura Sanay, Carmen Guaraca and Rosa Malan.*

RIGHT: *Lucia Guaman (left) wanted her daughter Monica to join the program to help her graduate high school, becoming her family's first female to earn a diploma.*

Campaigning for clean water in the name of their daughter

Parents and lifelong advocates partner with WE Charity to turn the taps on for the first time in their remote community in the Amazon.

Miguel Bargas welcomes visitors to his lush 79-acre farm in the Amazon rainforest by bearing fruit. He offers mouth-watering samples of the freshest mangos, papayas, bananas and oranges, all grown by him and picked that day. Before cutting them into bite-sized pieces, he rinses off any debris on the fruits' skin with water from a tap outside the front door of his house. It's a small gesture with weighted significance. Sitting on wooden benches in a shaded area, his wife, Maria, by his side, Miguel shares the family's story and reveals why water is so close to his heart. It began tragically in 2001 at the nearby Napo River.

An economic expressway, the river stretches more than 600 miles through the basin of the Amazon River. In places where marked roads are scarce, motorized canoes transport goods and ferry people to and from school, work and home, all the while seeping fuel into the waterway. Residents wash their clothes as fishermen bring in the daily catch, and neighborhood children bathe on shallow banks. For a long time "the highway," as Miguel calls it, was also the main source of drinking water for communities living along its shores, including 200 people from the Bargases' community of Mondaña.

Their daughter, 13-year-old Nelly Marcia, drank often from the dirty Napo. One day, she grew feverish. Miguel remembers tucking in their six children for the night, then dozing fitfully as their daughter's symptoms worsened. At midnight, both parents bundled their shivering child into a canoe and paddled the short distance across the river to a small health clinic that had few medications and limited resources for emergency care. Nelly Marcia was given two pills to take simultaneously and was then left under the close watch of her worried parents. Her symptoms continued to worsen, but there was nowhere else to take her at that time of night.

Just before sunup, less than 48 hours after her first signs of fever, Nelly Marcia passed away.

"It could have been because of the water and parasites," Miguel speculates in Spanish, his voice tight and monotone, barely above a whisper. "Maybe if the doctor had only

PILLAR

◊ WATER

Miguel and Maria Bargas: parents, fighters, clean-water champions
FOLLOWING SPREAD: *Maria and Miguel at the shoreline of the Napo River. Prior to the clean water project with WE Charity, contaminated river water devastated their family.*

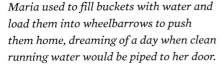
Maria used to fill buckets with water and load them into wheelbarrows to push them home, dreaming of a day when clean running water would be piped to her door.

prescribed one pill at a time, or there were better facilities." He trails off, softens. "I don't know. But that is what happened."

The rainforest's natural hum sits heavy in the air. When Miguel speaks again, his voice transitions back into its natural flow. He shares his family's tragedy as a landmark, a clear before-and-after that would mark his quest for clean water.

The exact cause of his daughter's death remains unknown, so Miguel focused on two facts he knew to be true—she drank unclean water, and his entire family was at risk of a similar fate.

Miguel saw signs of construction for industry development upstream, but no indications of a clean water system being built to serve Mondaña; bringing clean water to his community didn't seem to be anyone's priority. Although he lived in the Amazon rainforest surrounded by water, abundance was not the issue. His family members often fell ill from waterborne diseases caused by parasites and pollution in the waterways. The grieving father decided to advocate for the right to clean drinking water piped directly into homes in his community.

A farmer who rarely leaves his land, Miguel put on a clean shirt and dress pants—his city clothes—and took a half-hour canoe ride, then a five-hour bus ride over unpaved roads, to plead his case to municipal officials in Tena. In the nearest town, he asked the local

Maria harvesting crops on their 79-acre farm

government to provide a clean, reliable source of water in Mondaña. Miguel made this trip three times; each time, an official promised someone would visit his community and follow up. No one ever came.

"They never heard us," Maria underscores. For more than a decade the family awaited city officials while Maria continued to use jerry cans and a wooden wheelbarrow to haul river water to their home. Her husband helped her maneuver the heavy loads when it caused her too much pain. Meanwhile, Miguel kept advocating for their pipe dream, all the while worrying about the health of their children, who habitually suffered fevers, diarrhea and stomach cramps.

When WE Charity expanded its work from Ecuador's highlands to the Amazon area in 2013, one of the first people the country team met was Miguel.

Here Maria takes the lead: "One day we were chatting, like we are now. A man came here to the house and asked us, what are the needs of my family? So my husband answered. He said, 'It's water.'"

The country team was conducting needs assessments in communities along the Napo to develop sustainable solutions in partnership with the area's residents to address the most pressing problems.

New water piping winds its way through the Bargas farm, bringing clean water from a central storage tank through the family's cacao trees.

"I was very grateful, because going to advocate with the municipality was taking a lot of my effort and money," Miguel says. Suddenly he had an official ally. Mondaña was the first community in the Amazon to partner with WE Charity, starting with joint efforts to rebuild classrooms at the local school and then expanding into clean water projects. The local team showed Miguel they were serious from the beginning, hosting community-wide meetings to understand individual challenges before attempting solutions. Mondaña residents live on both sides of the Napo River, which would require separate water systems (tapping into different water sources, separate treatment tanks to purify the water, and individual storage tanks). It would take four miles of piping and many community volunteer days, known as mingas, to reach over 60 households.

While WE Charity courted donors to fund the new water projects in the Amazon, Miguel continued his role of advocate, this time rallying his neighbors to join in mingas to build the new water systems. He inspired his neighbors by telling them his truth: "Water is life."

His dedication was infectious.

Miguel's son became the project's foreman. Community members carried rocks and gravel to build the storage chamber's base and dug channels for pipes to connect to individual homes. Elders provided invaluable insight for the location of the filtration tanks,

to ensure they wouldn't wash away when major rains came. They remembered history's biggest storms; they knew the best land, no map or GPS needed.

Each side of the community fundraised 10 percent of its project's cost by tapping into government grants with WE Charity's support, while WE Charity donors covered the rest. The community investment was more than monetary; it built community owner-ship of the project and helped rural residents access the government programming available to them.

WE Charity completed two clean water systems in Mondaña in 2015. There's one to serve each side of the riverbank. Each has water piped from a freshwater spring to a filtration system, before making its way into neighborhood homes and the pri-mary school. Households pay a cost-per-use fee based on metering, managed by a community-elected Water Management Committee.

Miguel remembers the moment he finally turned on the tap beside his house, 14 years after his daughter's passing. "That day I felt something like I was dreaming. You know, what you don't see you can't believe, and I could barely believe what I was seeing."

After so many years of waiting, Miguel's hard work has the greatest payoff: "It's not only for us. It's for the future. For our grandsons and granddaughters. Now we sleep without worrying."

WANDA O'BRIEN

The water tap is just steps from the Bargases' front door, forever shifting the relationship the family has with this precious resource.

The Bargas family continues to farm fresh fruits, vegetables, coffee and cacao as they did before, but now the water surrounding them is no longer a threat. The next generation that farms the land will be free from the burden of worrying about water.

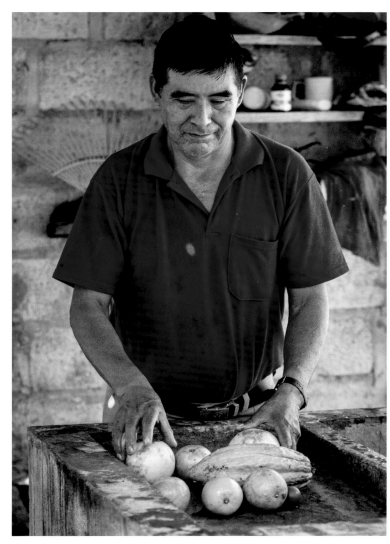

Lost, then found: Five generations fight for clean water

The Amazon rainforest is one of the wettest places on Earth, but for small riverside communities like Los Rios, clean water access is complicated. One family beat the odds.

As the matriarch of Los Rios, great-great-grandmother Rosa Ramos's official age may be unknown—she's been saying she's 98 for several years now—but the memory of her family's struggle to find clean water is clear.

Five generations of her family live within 10 feet of the Rio Humuyaku, which for many years threatened sickness with every sip. From her living-room window she can see it move lazily past, and her voice turns somber when she recalls the challenges her family has faced living in this riverside community in Ecuador's Amazon basin. "I never thought I'd see clean water here again in my lifetime."

At first the water in Los Rios was pristine. Rosa moved there in the 1970s at the beckoning of her eldest son, Hector, who now lives two houses over. The community was named after the province they migrated from, located hundreds of miles away on the other side of the country. Hector, one of the founding settlers, had left on an adventure from his coastal home as a young adult, crossing over the Andes mountain range and cutting his way through thick forest with a machete. He was part of a government program to decentralize densely populated regions, relocating farmers to uncultivated land. Once he found a place to farm, the rest of his family followed.

Los Rios's Rio Humuyaku feeds into the Napo River, the largest tributary leading to the Amazon River, which has the highest volume of water discharge in the world. Annual rainfall is as high as you'd imagine in a forested jungle region named after its rain.

The river water used to be glass-like, clear to look at and clean to drink. But as industries started to grow upriver and cities expanded, by the time the rushing waters reached Los Rios, the river held contaminants from human development and pollution. And though it frequently rains, catching rainwater is tricky. Even if enough rain is collected, heat, humidity and insects threaten the storage tanks.

Despite living in the rainforest surrounded by streams and rivers attached to the famed Amazon River, none was safe to drink from after decades of industry development. Rosa's mantra to her grandchildren and great-grandchildren became "Don't

PILLAR

⬥ WATER

Rosa Ramos: holder of memories, community matriarch

257

Viviana Veliz helps her grandmother Rosa with her daily chores. Prior to WE Charity installing the new water system, the entire community drank dirty river water.

drink the water" to avoid a roster of potentially deadly illnesses. All of their water, whether from the river or caught in buckets when the rain fell, had to be boiled before drinking.

"How many times did we go to the municipality to knock on the doors?" Rosa's son Hector asks rhetorically. Before local roads were built, his canoe ride to Tena, the closest city, took over eight hours. Even once roads were paved, the route still took hours by bus. Yet he made the journey countless times to petition the local government to bring clean drinking water to Los Rios. "And we never got a positive answer."

WE Charity started working in Ecuador's Amazon rainforest in 2013, starting with community outreach and needs assesments. Hector had one request when asked how the organization could help his community. "We were very direct. We said, 'We want water.'"

WE Charity hired a hydrologist to determine the most viable water source and worked with Los Rios residents to form a Water Management Committee. The community raised a percentage of the construction cost to demonstrate its ability to sustain the project. And Hector donated his own land, the site for a state-of-the-art filtration system beside the Rio Humuyaku.

Having access to clean water changes the details of daily life. A water tap beside the house makes everything easier, from doing laundry to washing dishes to making dinner. No more treks to the river.

Los Rios boasts a state-of-the-art filtration system, custom designed to remove pollutants that have contaminated the Amazon's waterways to create clean water for the community.

It's one of the most advanced treatment systems in the Amazon, a custom design from WE Charity built by Yakupro, a company based in the capital city of Quito, to serve this region of Ecuador, including over 70 families in Los Rios. Instead of water being collected directly from the river, it's now funneled through carefully monitored chemical filtrations to transform the polluted river water into clean drinking water.

Inside a chain-link enclosure littered with warning signs sits a vat 13 feet long, 7 feet wide and 6 feet high. It houses a series of eight compartments that force untreated water through a downward-tilting maze. From above, the vat looks a bit like a giant pinball machine. Compounds called flocculants, which attach to solid waste and cause it to sink, are injected into the first compartment and, as the mixture zigzags through its course, waste is dragged down and left at the bottom while the water moves on to the next compartment—where gravity continues its work. Outside the vat, in a separate tank, treated water is filtered again with a mix of activated charcoal to remove impurities and chlorine is added to kill parasites. After its journey and these few additives, the water is safe to consume.

The clean water is then pumped into three water towers, all built by WE Charity. There's enough pressure to supply clean water to the school and pipe it to every home in the community. The new water system has completely changed the relationship Hector, Rosa and their families have with this precious resource. "With complete trust we open the tap and we get enough water to prepare our food," Hector says. "We drink the water with no fear."

Rosa points to the contaminated water flowing past her window; "I thought that I would have to drink that water until the day I die." Instead, she takes a glass of clean water in her hand, brought by her granddaughter from the tap beside her house, and continues with a mischievous smile: "But I haven't died, and I'm drinking clean water."

KATIE HEWITT AND WANDA O'BRIEN

Hector Granja is a founder of Los Rios and community president many times over. A relentless advocate for clean water, he stands triumphantly in front of one of the three water towers that provide clean water to every household and the school in his community.

TOP: *Grandmother and granddaughter look out their window.*
RIGHT: *Students use the water station at Los Rios Primary School.*
FAR RIGHT: *Viviana washes dishes at home.*
FACING PAGE: *Rosa at home, a witness to the change that will benefit future generations*

The spirit of the *Samarina* lives on

A shipwrecked floating hospital and a crumbling clinic were calls to action. This is how WE Charity helped restore reliable, quality care to residents in remote rainforest communities.

Around a bend in the Napo River, a half-sunk ship protrudes from the water, a stark symbol of how fragile health care can be in villages along remote waterways in the Amazon jungle.

The relic is more than a marooned vessel; the double-decker boat once cruised the Napo as a floating hospital. Named *Samarina*, which means "healing" in the local Indigenous language, the government-operated ship provided much-needed health services to isolated communities along the riverbank in the Amazon rainforest. But in 2005, the engine malfunctioned. Neither the government nor the locals could invest the funds needed for repairs. The *Samarina* ceased operations. Later, when the Napo flooded, a fallen tree trunk delivered a knockout blow that sealed the ship's fate. Waterlogged, it settled as a half-sunk vestige, reminding all who passed of its failure to bring reliable health care to rural and Indigenous populations. Battered by the river, rain, humidity and time, the ship's name echoed what was both lost and so badly needed. Samarina.

While the stranded ship is a monument to health care challenges in a rainforest jungle, it was also an invitation. WE Charity first encountered the *Samarina* in 2012 and knew immediately it was too risky to launch another vessel. But they also found that the area's medical clinic on land wasn't faring much better.

A mile upstream from the wreck, Mondaña's derelict clinic was the sole source of nearby health care for 15 communities. It was built in the 1990s, and generations of termites had feasted on its infrastructure, threatening the integrity of the entire building. The jungle's damp air incubated mold, and bacteria were rife. Even the steps leading to the entrance were rotting planks that gave way under the feet of visiting patients. Government-assigned doctors from urban areas navigated the remote jungle clinic while trying to tend to the health concerns of patients. Despite their dedication, the quality of care was compromised.

In 2013, WE Charity started working with Mondaña on education and clean water projects, just as the local health clinic was set to close. Between the waterlogged boat

PILLAR

♥ **HEALTH**

Husband and wife Jose Shiguango and Rosa Andi stand with their grandson Mauricio. Jose is a healer and his wife is a midwife. They provide traditional health services to remote communities in the rainforest, but they also see the need for the comprehensive medical care that WE Charity has provided.

The once-floating Samarina *hospital symbolized the need for and challenge of providing reliable, quality health care in the Amazon.*

and the unstable clinic, Mondaña and its surrounding communities faced a health care crisis. So WE Charity, in partnership with Ecuador's Ministry of Health and the surrounding communities, set out to restore and improve access to health care with what would be the charity's largest project in Ecuador to date.

Designing quality health services in places where road access is limited and severe weather is constant is complicated. Still, lives depended on a solution. Without access to care, accidents and health hazards are magnified in one of Mother Nature's most humbling environments. Poisonous snakes and frogs are deadly. Common health ailments, like gastrointestinal illnesses, malnutrition, elevated blood-mercury levels, and vector-borne diseases, including dengue fever and malaria, are preventable and treatable, but only with proper services.

Maternal and child health is also threatened by isolation. Vaccinations are mandatory in Ecuador, but mothers with newborns avoided the dilapidated structure in Mondaña, not wanting to expose their children to its unsanitary environment. The only other option, a city hospital, was hours away by canoe or local bus, an investment of time and transport costs that many potential patients couldn't muster.

With all these urgent and preventable health challenges, local families depend on healers and shamans to ease pain and cure fever with natural ointments and potent teas, products of the largest tropical rainforest in the world, a biodiverse epicenter. Jose Shiguango, a respected traditional healer from Mondaña, has dedicated his life to curing his community, using the knowledge of his ancestors to extract medicinal properties from the rainforest's dense bush. When the ship and clinic were operating in peak condition, Jose saw the modern medicine as a complement to his own practice. When the ship sunk and the clinic rotted, even he felt the loss. After careful planning and community consultation, including input from Jose, WE Charity began the tricky construction project.

In the rainforest, roads are scarce; motorized canoes are used to transport supplies. Large construction equipment disrupts the ecosystem, so projects are built by hand. Weather can foil the best-laid plans.

In 2015, against the elemental odds, construction began. The old clinic was torn down and a new foundation was dug out of the earth, this one large enough to support rooms for emergency services, outpatient assessments, obstetrics, nursing and dentistry. Volunteers loaded bags of gravel, rocks and sand into motorized canoes to reach the construction site. On the day the foundation was to be laid, storm clouds threatened to wash away precious materials, but a minga brought more than 100 volunteers from communities as far away as 40 minutes upriver to help. By sunset, the foundation was laid.

Momentum at the build site continued over many months. A human chain loaded 600 bricks twice a week into a waiting canoe. Over 10,000 bricks crossed the river to build clinic walls that could withstand the heat and humidity. With the structure set, the clinic's insides started to arrive, boat by boat. A 13-foot-tall refrigerator for vaccines, a dental chair and several clinic beds all had to be wrestled into canoes.

On the clinic's official opening day in June 2016, the sky opened. But the roof didn't leak; visitors didn't slip on the floorboards; and instead of avoiding the previous unsanitary conditions, residents from up and down the Napo arrived to officially celebrate the opening of something they never thought they'd see—an advanced medical facility in the middle of the jungle. Just as the ceremony began, the sun broke through the clouds. Even Mother Nature seemed to be celebrating.

With the new clinic as a base of operations, health care once again went on the move to reach distant communities. A medical brigade—comprising the clinic's doctor, nurse, dentist, and health technician and WE Charity's health coordinator—loads vaccines and necessary supplies into a motorized canoe to reach their shores, setting up makeshift exam rooms in schools to provide health care to students, young families and elderly residents. The promise of samarina has come full circle.

WANDA O'BRIEN

ABOVE: *Modern medicine complements the knowledge and practice of traditional healers, such as Jose Shiguango (right), to provide holistic care to patients.*
FOLLOWING SPREAD: *Sand is hauled into a waiting canoe. Constructing the new Mondaña Health Clinic in the rainforest required many mingas, countless canoe trips and lots of helpful hands.*

The new Mondaña Health Clinic is nestled along the shoreline of the Napo River. The clinic serves the surrounding communities and acts as a base camp for medical staff who travel to more remote areas to provide health care.

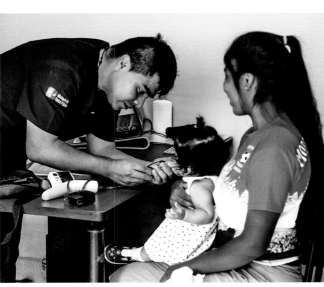

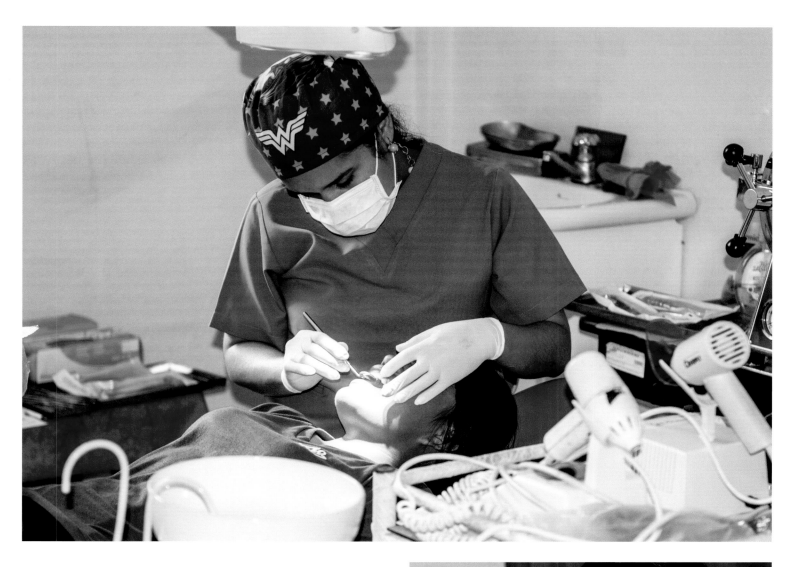

FACING PAGE: *Dentist Franciarge Mucura Monteverde treats patients of all ages, putting to good use state-of-the-art equipment that was wrestled onto canoes and through the jungle to end up in the clinic.*
THIS PAGE: *Maternal and child health is a primary focus of the clinic, in addition to general outpatient and dental services.*

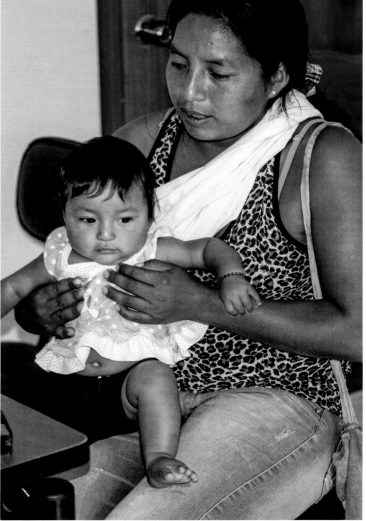

A garden at the edge of the world

High in the Chimborazo mountains, a small school plot feeds hundreds.

With stubborn grit, Shuid Primary School students tug at stalks of cilantro and ripe radishes that burst from the ground like leafy green fountains. Their faces are strained; the roots are deep. Determined, the agro-apprentices wrestle with their prizes until the earth loosens its hold on the plants. Shaking off the dirt, the students present their bouquets.

Shuid is nestled on a ridge at the end of a switchback mountain road in Ecuador's Chimborazo province. The school campus and surrounding community sit 12,000 feet above sea level. Some days, a late morning fog rolls in and erases the horizon, making it look like a village at the edge of the world.

Most of the students' parents are farmers on unforgiving land. On high-altitude farms, erosion, low-nutrient soil and uneven terrain complicate production, especially irrigation. Few crop varieties are hardy enough to withstand high winds and erratic weather. Farming is still necessary for survival in the remote mountains, where strong rains or falling rocks can cut off supply routes.

Shuid's students, including high schooler Laura Sanay, are growing their own food in a thriving garden, learning tricks that even their parents don't know.

Shuid's school garden traces its roots to 2017, when the first starter plants from WE Charity were bedded. Agriculture studies are now ingrained in the curriculum. WE Charity helps implement the program with training in best practices for small farms. Laura and her classmates then share the lessons in their parents' fields, improving family harvests as well as enhancing their own future prospects. It can be tempting to pull children from class and have them work on a struggling family farm, but Shuid's parents can appreciate the value of an education that also helps their crops. The school's agriculture program is an incentive to keep kids in school, where they gain practical knowledge that benefits entire households. Once their family's fields and finances improve, children have more choices after high school graduation. Little gardeners also grow awareness for WE Charity's other offerings. Both Laura's mother and her aunt signed up for the organization's Healthy Families program, home hygiene and nutrition lessons designed to improve health.

PILLAR

◆ FOOD

Kindergarten students from Shuid Primary School will grow up with WE Charity's school garden program. Most families in the mountainous region of Chimborazo are subsistence farmers who struggle to grow crops from poor-quality soil. The agricultural training students receive at school finds its way back to their parents' fields.

The whole community of Shuid rallied to start the garden. Black soil, a more nutrient-dense composition, had to be shipped from another region. A truck hauled in bags and everyone dispersed the dirt, now cultivated into rows of carrots, zucchini, purple cabbage, red onions, beets, kale, turnips and corn—much more crop variety than in local farmers' plots.

Mario Mulum is only 12, but he's already taught his parents a few things. From WE Charity's food program coordinator, he learned how to maneuver a bucket or a hose for more targeted irrigation. He brought the methods home and his parents listened.

Mario ponders for a moment and decides beets are the best, his favorite dish served at school feasts. A big harvest can feed the whole school, nearly 400 students, plus teachers, on special occasions. In 2018, Día del Niño, or Children's Day, was celebrated with potato soup and chicken stew, plus a good mix of veggies. And there were leftovers for each family.

If Shuid's students continue to bring home farming lessons, this one small school garden will feed a whole community for years to come.

KATIE HEWITT

ABOVE: *Laura (far left) stands with her extended family in their home garden. Good nutrition has become a family affair; her mom and aunt joined WE Charity's Healthy Families program, where they learn healthy food and hygiene habits to practice at home.*
FACING PAGE, TOP: *Grade 7 students tend to Shuid's school garden. Students learn to cultivate a wide variety of crops in the harsh high altitude that challenges many local farmers.*
BOTTOM LEFT: *The garden benefits all grades. High schooler Laura Sanay (middle) stands between her grandmother and aunt. Laura often brings home the farming techniques she learns at school.*
BOTTOM RIGHT: *Mario Mulum, 12, holds a fresh bunch of cilantro. The garden program improves harvests, household incomes and the students' prospects after graduation.*

A cacao graveyard comes back to life

The WE Agricultural Learning Center helps rural farmers revive failing crops.

Raul Alvarado grew up among cacao trees, shadowing his father to learn their mysterious habits until the trees outgrew them both. Eventually their crops were too tall to harvest. Father and son couldn't reach the leathery oblong pods that hung from high branches.

Like many smallholder farmers in Ecuador's Amazon basin, Raul's father didn't have the skills or the means to care for the notoriously finicky cacao. Colonial rule had isolated rural families from the best plots, market access and formal agricultural training for centuries, turning regional farms into ad hoc means of survival. In an innovative industry there is room for risk, to experiment with new methods when old ones fail. But for Raul's family, risk meant struggle and the loss of vital income. His father decided to cut his losses and cull his cacao fields, destroying what could have been a lucrative business.

Hiding inside those pods just out of reach were cacao beans that, once fermented and dried, are essential for chocolate production and a key ingredient in the multibillion-dollar industry. With skilled care, cacao trees flourish in the damp, fertile Amazon and its stable climate, where evidence suggests humans first consumed chocolate thousands of years ago.

Cacao has been growing in the region for centuries, but modern rural farmers are struggling with the art and science of cultivation. "We are farmers," said Raul, "but we are blind without training."

No longer a boy, Raul has children of his own. He rhymes off their names, 11 of them, adding proudly that they all attend school at his insistence. After working odd jobs and coming up short, he returned to his roots and planted his own cacao crop to support his big family in the small community of Cruz Chicta. Nothing grew. "We didn't know how to take care of it," he said through a translator. The trees rotted, and Raul abandoned them.

Maybe Raul is more stubborn than his father—with the memory of two failed fields, he decided to try once more. This time, he planned to seek out expert help.

PILLAR

◆ FOOD

Farmers in Ecuador's Napo province struggle to care for cacao, a finicky crop that takes years to mature. But with proper cultivation, their fields hold the key ingredient of the multibillion-dollar chocolate industry.

ABOVE: *Raul Alvarado has been farming cacao since he was a boy, without much success. He attended the first-ever training session at WE's Agricultural Learning Center to boost his harvest in order to provide for his 11 children.*

ABOVE RIGHT: *The WE Agricultural Learning Center is a sprawling 170-acre campus along the Napo River. A demonstration field is divided among farmers, who practice their trimming, irrigation and other techniques on their assigned plants.*

FACING PAGE, TOP: *Cacao pods hold beans that, once fermented and dried, are the key ingredient in chocolate production.*

FACING PAGE, BOTTOM: *Melquiades Coello, head instructor at the WE Agricultural Learning Center, is known as the "cacao engineer."*

His young plants, distributed to Cruz Chicta farmers as part of a government program, had just settled into the ground when the news reached him that WE's Agricultural Learning Center had opened and would host its first cacao training for local farmers. He couldn't believe his good fortune. WE Charity mobilizers had been spreading word of the training for weeks, encouraging local leaders to pass on the news.

"It was an act of God," Raul said.

For local farmers, growing cacao is frustrating, particular and exacting. It takes years of cultivation before the first fruit blossoms, a long stretch to wait for farmers with limited acreage. Most have fields that span just a quarter or half hectare. This makes cacao a risky investment when less temperamental crops, such as maize, could flourish. Failing cacao is quickly abandoned to make room for simpler, more immediate solutions. But cacao can also bring great rewards. Ecuador's offering to the global chocolate market is premium.

A readily available variety called CCN51 is a genetically modified crop from Ecuador's government, the kind that Raul and many others planted as part of an incentive program. Many major chocolate brands buy these plentiful beans to satisfy huge production quantities. Growing CCN51 can be good business for a diligent farmer willing to learn.

The country's national cacao, *fino de aroma*, is Ecuador's darling crop, waiting to satisfy the cravings of more discerning palates. The international award–winning variety is ranked high for its flavor, aroma and rarity on the world market. With buyers willing to pay premium prices for the national cacao, Ecuador's rural farmers are sitting on potential goldmines. In many places in the Amazon, *fino de aroma* grows naturally, but it frequently dies without proper cultivation.

WE's Agricultural Learning Center is built over a cacao graveyard. Now the center brings new life, helping Raul and other local farmers fill the knowledge gap for both crop varieties with agricultural best practices in irrigation, pruning, spacing and optimal sun exposure. A state-of-the-art classroom and 170-acre demonstration field host regular training sessions. Each participating farmer is assigned four trees in the practice field to care for over several months, under supervision from WE Charity's trainers. They're led by head instructor Melquiades Coello, known affectionately as the "cacao engineer" for devoting his life to the plant and its quirks.

Melquiades says the local farmers' prevailing instincts are to let Mother Nature take over, to watch as branches flex to the sky and leaves crowd each other. Many farmers don't realize they are committing arboreal sin. Cacao trees need to be scaled back, like bonsai trees. Trimming is so crucial that it's the first hands-on lesson in the training program.

TOP: *Raul Alvarado practices the proper technique for pruning cacao trees at WE's Agricultural Learning Center.*
BOTTOM: *Fresh branch cuts are sealed with a compound of minerals to protect the tree from disease.*

With trimming, more light reaches the fruit and eases harvesting. Farmers no longer need to climb to the top of high trees to reach cacao pods, which was dangerous and time consuming: there are few ladders in the remote jungle.

Raul was a vocal student, eager to share and answer questions in the classroom portion before he moved on to the real thing, the real soil, the real trees.

He and 60 classmates traipsed through the jungle to reach the farm, where cacao pods hung on branches trimmed back to manageable heights. Raul eagerly used his own pruning tool to practice cutting off a few branches, just as Melquiades had shown him.

Raul thought back to his father's trees and their impossibly high branches. It was a lesson 40 years in the making. "I'm going to apply everything I've learned," he said of his own field. Never again will he abandon mature trees, he said, which he'd done regularly before. Instead, he'll keep trimming them back, increasing his crop yields and his income—for his kids and their school fees.

Raul is now a cacao ambassador, encouraging others to join the training. He's already recruited dozens of other farmers from Cruz Chicta to share in the lessons at the Agriculture Learning Center. Farming is a big responsibility that he wants to ensure his fellow farmers take seriously. "We are the ones who feed the people. We are responsible for our own work."

KATIE HEWITT

TOP: *Cacao pods contain luscious white fruit that encases the precious beans. Once the pods are cracked open, the cacao beans are fermented and dried in preparation for chocolate production.*
ABOVE: *ME to WE's Fair Trade chocolate contains beans grown by WE Charity's partners, smallholder cacao farmers on the Ecuadorian coast.*

When the ordinary is extraordinary

Life looks different in Bellavista, where a group of women artisans overcame resistance, waited for a full moon and conquered self-doubt to become as strong as possible.

Like the thatched roof that covers the artisan *choza* built by their own hands, the changes in Bellavista's women since they formed an all-female group are textured, layered and long-lasting.

Olga Shiguango is a founding member of the women's group, located in a community accessed only by canoe or a bone-shaking dirt road that cuts through the rainforest jungle. Employment opportunities are scarce. Olga's income came from farming plantain, corn, coffee and cacao, but she had a small plot of land and unreliable access to market. In 2014, WE Charity—already building new classrooms for the community's local school—established the group to help women earn an income through traditional weaving practices and to support female leaders determined to make a change in their community.

Building the choza was the group's first act of independence. The women desired a place they could call their own, to fulfill orders, host workshops and gather together. Olga and her comrades insisted on being the core construction crew, and they reversed gender roles by recruiting their husbands as help. Many of those men initially resisted their wives' joining an all-women collective, but once they saw the financial impact of the program, they offered their support and their muscle.

The women wove the choza roof out of the Amazon's *paja toquilla*, palm leaves that folklore dictates should be cut only under a full moon if they are to remain durable. The women walked miles into the jungle at night to harvest the supply. After threading the leaves into roofing sheets, they passed them up to their husbands to secure in place.

For Olga, as for her neighbors living in this small community on the shores of the Napo River, the personal impact of belonging to the group has transformed even the smallest details of daily life. "I have peace of mind, and I don't worry anymore about how to feed my family," says Olga, who sits on a bench in the shade of the open-air artisan workspace she helped build. "When my daughter comes home from school and wants a snack, I can tell her to go to the local shop and get one. I tell her, 'Put it on my credit. I have money. I can pay for that.'"

Olga Shiguango is a founding member of Sumak Warmi, a name selected by the artisans group— and Kichwa for "beautiful women."

Lidia Tapuy creates string from the fibers of the Amazon pita leaf.

287

TOP: *Priscila Andy, group vice president, leads a discussion. Beyond making artisan jewelry, group members also participate in financial literacy and leadership workshops.*

ABOVE: *Leaves harvested under moonlight were used for the choza's thatched roof; they promise strength and durability.*

A few times a week, Olga joins more than a dozen artisans in the space to weave bracelets out of fibers torn from long pita leaves that grow in the Amazon rainforest. The women chat and laugh as they work, their movements second nature. They also sew wallets and purses out of recycled wrappers and plastic bags. These handicrafts are sold at ME to WE's Minga Lodge to visitors, who also meet with the women to learn about their culture and way of life.

Olga explains that her husband, Saul, unlike many of the other men, has been her biggest supporter. Although she has become a skilled artisan, the journey was filled with trepidation. "At first I didn't know if I could do it," she confesses. Though a high school graduate, she had no previous experience with weaving, aside from the training provided by WE Charity. She worried she was too slow and would never make a bracelet properly. She almost gave up. "My husband told me, 'I think you can do it. You just have to work hard and show others what you can do.'"

Group members who didn't receive support at home found it in each other. Priscila Andy, the group's vice president, explains that women whose sole focus was household chores and who rarely spoke in public became more ambitious, independent and self-assured. "Now we can speak our minds and we support each other with our ideas," she says.

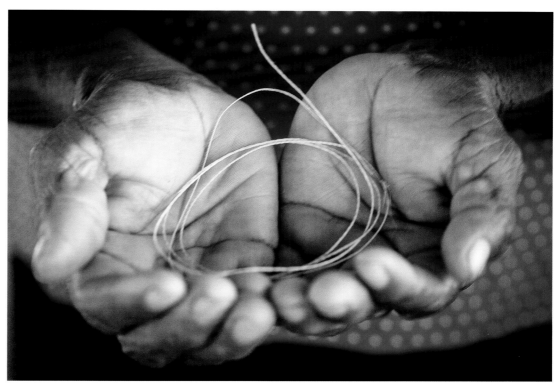

The pita leaf is separated from top to bottom to extract hidden fibers, then it is dried, dyed and woven into jewelry.

Behind every piece of jewelry from the Bellavista women's group is the story of the woman who wove it—artisans, farmers and mothers who are committed to creating a better life for themselves and their families.

TOP ROW: *Marlene Shiguango, Violeta Grefa, Graciela Shiguango, Olga Shiguango, Rita Grefa, Lucia Andy*

BOTTOM ROW: *Zoila Andy, Solange Shiguango, Flora Grefa, Ana Tapuy, Priscila Andy*

WE Charity has also run financial literacy, small business management and leadership workshops. Olga's confidence grew and she was elected the group's treasurer, putting her high school diploma to good use. The financial management training she received not only helped her keep the group's books in order, it also improved her household budgeting.

The first time Olga completed an order for 100 bracelets, she finally believed she could make a living as an artisan. She's put her pay packages toward food, clothes, school supplies and medicines. After the essentials were covered, she made her first large purchase: a fridge. She's also set aside savings for her children's education.

When Olga weaves at home, her daughter, Dayana, often joins her, fashioning her own creations out of string and beads. Olga watches with the quiet pride of a working mom.

WANDA O'BRIEN

TOP, LEFT TO RIGHT: *ME to WE finds market access for the group's handmade jewelry; Olga oversees her daughter studying.*
ABOVE: *Olga with her niece Clara (far left, holding her nephew Claudio), daughter Dayana and son Jair.*

Infrastructure in Ecuador

Beneath the inspirational stories of transformation in Ecuador's Chimborazo and Napo provinces that this book celebrates are the concrete foundations upon which so much of WE Charity's work is built. This infrastructure includes state-of-the-art water systems, classrooms outfitted with desks and computers, a medical clinic, and training spaces tailored to support the skills of artisans and farmers.

WE Charity supporters not only fund transformative programs that help families in creating their own solutions to end poverty, they also come together to finance the construction of significant infrastructure projects.

Handwashing station at a primary school in the Amazon

The blueprints for a state-of-the-art water filtration system in the Amazon

New high school in Chimborazo

Primary classroom in Gulag

Cacao trees surround the chocolate laboratory at WE's Agricultural Learning Center.

Mondaña Health Clinic provides primary care to rural communities.

High school students use their new computer lab

The first classroom WE Charity built in the community of San Miguel in Chimborazo.

Students in front of their classroom in the community of Hatun Urku in the Amazon.

WE's work around the world

Since its founding in 1995, WE Charity has built schoolrooms in more than 45 countries around the world. As the organization moved toward its five-pillar approach to sustainable development, it focused its efforts in specific countries to create the greatest impact from donor dollars. In addition to India, Kenya and Ecuador, WE Charity also operates in rural China, Ethiopia, Haiti, Nicaragua, Sierra Leone and Tanzania. The following pages celebrate some of the incredible achievements in each of these countries, none of which would have been possible without supporters committed to creating a world free of child labor, where families have the resources to invest in their children's futures.

The Wenjia school campus

Students in front of their school in Aluo

Sheep are an important part of the animal husbandry program

Medical camp in action

Tao Shui school

Clean water system in Quanyuan

CHINA

WE Charity began development work in rural China in 2002, following news of a tragic explosion in a fireworks factory, where 38 children were killed. Knowing those children died because they were forced to work rather than go to school, WE Charity partnered with communities and the local government to help break the cycle of poverty and transform access to education in remote areas of the country.

A new water system

Primary school campus set in the valley of the Tigray region

Students at a new classroom in Alose

Girls collect clean water

Students celebrate the inauguration of their new school in Garora

New classroom block in Awash Kolati

Inside a new classroom in Garora

ETHIOPIA

In 2017, WE Charity expanded into Ethiopia by partnering with Canadian-based non-profit imagine1day to continue to bring quality education to the Tigray and Oromia regions of the country. In addition to building new schoolrooms and water projects, WE Charity is expanding the development work to include food security and financial opportunities.

A new classroom in Marialapa

School lunches served in Dos Palais

The Dos Palais campus. Every grade selects the color of their classroom.

Inside a new classroom

The first classroom built in Kabayi

Women receive their goats in Marialapa as part of an income-generating program.

HAITI

WE Charity's work in Haiti, which began in 2000, stands out in the country because of its guiding principle of finding sustainable solutions. WE Charity deepened its work in the Caribbean country in 2010, when Haiti was hit by a devasting earthquake. Despite the environmental challenges that continue to befall the country, WE Charity sees tremendous success in rural communities in the Central Plateau region, where the organization is focused on removing obstacles that prevent children from getting access to a quality education.

Medical camp in action

Preschool classroom in El Trapiche

Recycled tires are used to build the school gardens.

New classrooms in San Marcos

New library in San Diego

Balloons decorate the schoolyard to celebrate the first classroom built in El Trapiche.

NICARAGUA

WE Charity started to work in Nicaragua in 1998, by constructing or rehabilitating schools across the country. It has since built clean water systems, provided essential preventative health training, created school gardens and invested in the entrepreneurial spirit of women through a thriving artisan program, all of which are focused on keeping children in the classroom.

El Trapiche students in front of their new school

Goat rearing is part of the animal husbandry program

Hard-of-hearing school for Ebola survivors

Primary school students in Kono District

Girls skip rope and play soccer during recess at Moyamba school

Students on the playground of their new school

SIERRA LEONE

WE Charity has worked in Sierra Leone since the end of the country's civil war in 2002, and is committed to creating the brightest future for its youth. With more than half of the country's population illiterate, WE Charity is focused on removing the barriers to education, and it partners with a local organization to implement clean water, health and income-generating projects, in addition to improving school infrastructure.

Laboratory at Engikaret Secondary School

Clean water flows from a water tap

Namelok Primary School

Engutukoiti Primary School

Orbomba Primary School

Community members and parents at Oldonyowas Primary School

Students inside Oldonyowas Primary School

TANZANIA

In 2002, after the Tanzanian government eliminated primary school fees, WE Charity began partnering with educators, community leaders and the local government to improve school infrastructure and increase the number of qualified teachers. WE Charity also provides clean water, health, food security and opportunity programming to remove the many obstacles to education.

Personal Perspectives: WE Charity champions share their journeys of inspiration

Phoebe Rotman: Student, volunteer and entrepreneur

I'll never forget the first time I went on a ME to WE Trip to Kenya with my family, when I was 12. I thought I knew what to expect, but my only experience of the country had been the narrow, distorted images of Africa I'd seen on TV. My trip to Kenya altered that perspective, and I'm so grateful for all the ways it changed my life.

There was a bit of culture shock at first. I was struck by the extreme poverty I saw in some communities—the poor living conditions, the crumbling school buildings. Even with the efforts of the global community, many people are still stuck in these circumstances. But the more time I spent getting to know the Maasai and Kipsigis people WE Charity works with, the more I admired their immense resilience and was moved by their drive to educate their children so they would have more opportunities.

I also related to them on an interpersonal level.

My great-grandfather, Manny Rotman, worked his way up from nothing. He escaped persecution in Poland and came to Canada in 1927 unable to speak English and built several businesses up from scratch. I saw the same kind of drive that my great-grandfather had in the people of Melelo, a rural Kenyan village. They are so resourceful. I wanted to support them as they strive to create better lives for their families by focusing on WE Charity's opportunity pillar.

When I returned home to Toronto, I was preparing to become a bat mitzvah, which meant I was becoming a woman in my own Jewish culture. This got me thinking about all the girls I'd met in Melelo and how limited their opportunities were compared with mine, which are so open because of where I live. I wanted to do something to support and honor them as they became women in their culture— to find a way to use what I'd been learning about ME to WE's social enterprise model. I came up with the idea of combining something traditionally worn in my culture with something traditionally worn in Maasai communities.

I'd seen the beautiful beaded Rafiki bracelets being made by the Maasai mamas in Melelo. The women then sold them to earn money for their families, earning a sustainable source of income by working with ME to WE. So I approached the mamas and asked if they could also bead kippahs, the small skullcaps traditionally worn by Jewish men. I thought if I could help market new products—Rafippahs—on their behalf in North America, it would give them a bit more work.

I also felt the project highlighted the similarities between Maasai culture and my own culture—the fact that we share the same core values of community, charity and taking care of one another.

I named the beaded kippahs "Rafippahs" after doing a bit of marketing research, and started selling them online. I'm now proud to say that I work with the mamas and families of Melelo. After the business launched, with support from my family and friends, I was lucky enough to return to visit Melelo on a ME to WE youth trip.

ABOVE: *Phoebe Rotman with Kitiringa Keiwua, a member of the women's opportunity group in Melelo, Kenya*
FACING PAGE: *ME to WE travelers gain insight into global water issues and learn from local residents while on a water walk in Kenya.*

While there, I was invited to the home of a 12-year-old girl named Vicki. I went with her on the long walk she would take each day to fetch water for her family from a distant river. Despite our obvious cultural differences and a bit of a language barrier, Vicki and I had a lot in common. We both shared a love of writing and music. When I met her mother, Eleanor, she told me that the money she'd earned from beading items, including Rafippahs, had provided her with new opportunities. She could buy food, goats for milk, and pay for Vicki's school fees, which would enable Vicki to become the first person in her family to get a high school education.

A portion of the profits from Rafippahs will also be used to fund a Women's Empowerment Centre in Melelo, where the mamas will be able to gather to bead together, share stories and feel a sense of community. While I'm focusing on WE Charity's opportunity pillar,

my two brothers are raising funds to bring education and clean water to Melelo.

My trip to Kenya taught me a lot and inspired me to gain even more knowledge. I'm still researching the effects of globalization, and all the issues surrounding international development. The next time I visit Melelo, Vicki and I can share what we've learned with each other.

Rosie Pesek: Teacher, traveler and activist

When I was in high school, my teacher took a group of us to volunteer in Oaxaca, Mexico. The lesson that's stayed with me, all these years later, is to bring my activism with me no matter where I end up. That philosophy took me to El Salvador to volunteer at an orphanage and to Chile to work alongside teachers and social workers in classrooms. When I returned to the United States to become a history and civics teacher, I wanted to bring social justice into my classroom and motivate my students to be of service to others. That desire led me to WE.

I went with other educators from across the United States and Canada on a ME to WE Trip to Ecuador to see and volunteer for WE Charity's five-pillar development model. A few days into my trip, I was reminded of that lesson from years ago—and became even more determined to view the world, and the problems we tackle in my classroom, through a different lens.

ABOVE: *Rosie Pesek (right) and her colleague Renae Stone in 2016 at the build site in Bellavista, Ecuador*
FACING PAGE: *Minga Lodge is ME to WE's base for travelers in Ecuador. Built in harmony with the environment, the thoughtfully designed rooms back onto the biodiverse Amazon rainforest.*

During our time together, we educators discussed development issues while snaking our way by canoe along the Napo River in the Amazon basin, past communities hugging the shoreline or emerging from the rainforest. We wielded shovels to clear the foundation for a library and carried bricks to build its walls. And we spent hours reflecting on our roles in shaping young minds.

But it wasn't until we were sitting in a circle, knee-to-knee with community members and elders from the village of Bellavista, listening as they talked about their vision for the future, that it dawned on me: I wanted my students to experience this. I needed to bring them to Ecuador.

When I got back to Chicago, I immediately started planning my next trip, where I would take my students from John F. Kennedy High School. We immediately set up a WE club and my 14- and 15-year-old students began studying development issues and fundraising for a trip. Less than a year after my time in Ecuador, I was back in the Amazon with five young women from my class.

I'll never forget how eager my girls were to reach the build site that first day. We were in the village of Kanambu to help build a new classroom for the school, which was overflowing. It was hard work. The first day, my students weren't mentally prepared for it, tiring themselves out in excitement. It wasn't as if I was just watching them, mind you. I was busy filling barrels with rocks and bending rebar right next to them. It was hot. It was challenging. And it was worth all the effort to get there.

Every night after the build, we'd take time to reflect. It was an emotional experience for some, a spiritual one for others. But for all of them there was a *wow* moment, an instant that crystallized their new global perspective. No matter the differences in geography or language, the things we share in common across cultures are much more powerful. They saw the young community members we met in the rainforest or along the Napo thirsting for an education, and my students recommitted themselves to their own future. They began to see the connections between themselves and global issues and to lead with compassion.

When we returned to Chicago, my students shone. They settled into their new roles as leaders, more confident in themselves and their place in the world. I have always tried to inspire the young girls and boys in my classroom to be of service. That's what my experiences volunteering abroad did for me. And that's what our time with WE in Ecuador did for my students.

Kim Plewes:
Anti-child-labor activist, WE Charity champion and advocate

I vividly remember the day I learned that the clothes I was wearing, the carpets I walked on and the food I ate might be made by children my age, slaving half the world away. I was sitting in my Grade 6 classroom as my teacher took a few minutes to read us stories of kids who weren't lucky enough to be sitting in their own classroom, counting the minutes until lunch break.

In 1998, friends and I started a petition against child labor, and as we gathered signatures, we were bullied and ostracized at school for our efforts. Six months in, we heard about a teenage anti-child-labor activist coming to our town. We bought tickets. It was Craig Kielburger.

As he spoke on stage about what had inspired him to start WE Charity (then Free The Children) and his travels to meet these kids firsthand, I knew I had found my people. Here was someone who didn't just get it—he was doing something about it. He not only signed our petition, he helped get it introduced in the House of Commons in front of the prime minister and the full Canadian Parliament.

My first paid job with WE was working as front desk receptionist. I've since had many other responsibilities, from opening a new regional office in the US to helping families realize their philanthropic goals through their support of WE Charity. I've co-led our 20th and 25th anniversary fundraising campaigns.

I've also traveled to more than 65 countries. My first trip was to rural Nicaragua, where we had built our first school. Six hours away from basic road access, I helped build new classrooms. Whenever I visit the rural communities where WE works, I try to spend time with local families. I leave realizing we are far more similar than we are different. We face the same struggles and share similar dreams. I am privileged to spend my life helping to alleviate their burdens so they can accomplish their dreams.

Our five-pillar sustainable development model is not about handouts, but handups. It's about empowerment and capacity building. It's about creating agency. This book, which I am proud to have helped bring to life, presents a handful of stories that showcase that agency. Change doesn't happen fast. And sometimes it's minuscule. But every step is a step in the right direction.

As I return to Kenya year after year, those steps add up to profound change. One of my favorite stories (and you can see the women's photos earlier in this book) is of the Winning Women's Group in Melelo, Kenya. I got to know these 15 remarkable women, all part of one extended family, as we sat together beside their mud-and-stick homes. There were kids playing in the background, babies crying and dozens of neighbors wandering by, intrigued by my visit.

These Maasai women must rely on their family's herd of cattle to survive. Their husbands often move with the herds for weeks or months at a time, searching for greener pastures to ensure the herd's survival, leaving their wives to maintain the homestead, raise the kids and take care of any small crops that have been planted.

These hardworking mamas, all between the ages of 17 and 40, shared with me the struggles of covering daily household expenses, whether purchasing a new bar of soap for washing or some salt to flavor meals. After suffering for years, unable to cover those expenses, the women came together with the support of WE Charity to form a group, choosing the name "winning" because they hoped that by working together and sharing their tools and resources, they would become winners! They've started small businesses and now earn the income needed to replace the bar of soap or buy more salt.

I remember when one woman, Nkoje, a shy mother of 10 children, leaned forward and proudly whispered to me, "I can now do something to provide the small things that my family needs. I don't need to wait for my husband to return. We are very joyful and happy to be able to solve our own problems!" If that isn't the living embodiment of a woman experiencing the feeling of empowerment, I don't know what is!

LEFT: *Kim Plewes with members of the Winning Group, a women's opportunity collective in Melelo, Kenya*
FACING PAGE: *The dining platform at Bogani, ME to WE's accommodation in Kenya's Maasai Mara, invites guests to share stories and reflect on their day while enjoying meals.*

Craig Burkinshaw:
Expert traveler, entrepreneur and WE Charity board member

When I first heard about WE Villages, I was a bit skeptical. Like most Brits, I had a sense that international development work can be done very poorly, and few people get the chance to see it in person, so most rely on secondhand accounts. I admit that news stories of corruption and irresponsible practices at other charities had given me a bad view of the sector.

Then, late in 2012, I had the chance to go to Kenya with ME to WE Trips, on the recommendation of a friend. My company, Audley Travel, already had me thinking about new angles on sustainable tourism. Audley has sent tens of thousands of people on tailor-made trips all over the world, the kind of cultural immersion that isn't offered elsewhere. I started Audley in 1996, and I've traveled the globe. Having seen so much of the world, I felt I could be doing more to give back to it. I boarded another plane, this time bound for Kenya.

In the Maasai Mara, I visited WE Charity's water projects, always installed near reconstructed school buildings so that girls could collect clean water on their way home. I walked through school gardens that fed students and I visited health clinics, taking in the holistic model and its five distinct, yet interconnected, pillars. To keep track of progress across multiple facets, there are detailed metrics for success and third-party verification reports (which I later read, by the way, quite thoroughly). It was a lot to take in. I found WE Charity's model to be complex on first contact—especially under the Kenyan sun while jet-lagged. I was used to TV adverts about water charities that only delivered clean water, which was simpler, but not enough. WE Charity has a multifaceted approach for very good reasons. The problems aren't simple. Why would the solutions be?

I started working with ME to WE Trips in the hardest-hit rural areas of developing countries, to bring more people to witness a successful development model in person. There's more than one way to get under the skin of a place, and ME to WE Trips has done it brilliantly. You learn about daily life in these areas in a way that isn't possible with other kinds of travel. And every ME to WE trip directly supports WE Charity projects.

I've since been back to Kenya with ME to WE several times, and to Ecuador and India. In the middle of the savanna, the Amazon rainforest and the foothills of Rajasthan's Aravalli mountain range, you'll find little oases in ME to WE's lodgings, bespoke designs by local architects that preserve the environment. In Ecuador, Minga Lodge sits on the shore of the Napo River, which feeds into the Amazon. Just across the river are homes and schools and farms that belong to WE Charity's partner communities.

On one of my trips to India, I met a group of farmers. I was interested in all the minute details—the increased harvest yields and supplementary crop varieties that came with WE Charity's food security pillar—but struck most by a casual comment. One farmer told me that while his health and nutrient intake had improved, his wife was also experimenting with the cooking, making tastier and more varied meals. That was the best part, he said. It was such a simple thing. These are the kinds of stories you'll read about in this book, little moments of impact that help make an intricate system come to life.

Shortly after my first trip to Kenya, I was invited to join WE Charity's UK Board of Directors. I'd seen the work, and I was all in. I'm still passionate about WE Charity's model and ME to WE travel, but most of all, I'm passionate about getting the word out, especially to skeptics like me.

ABOVE: *Craig Burkinshaw balances a clay pot to help carry water in Rajasthan, India.*
FACING PAGE: *Araveli, ME to WE's camp in India, celebrates Rajasthani architecture and the local landscape. The dining platform provides spectacular views of India's oldest mountain range.*

Peter Cordy:
Volunteer, supporter and photographer

I used to believe that the world was a dark place, but now I know that I was naïve. In the years that I have worked with WE Charity, I've had the pleasure of supporting a number of international development projects, and I have seen how much good we can do even with the smallest actions. So many of the organization's supporters, whether schoolchildren or CEOs, are guided by the same perspective. When I travel to visit our partner communities and see the impact of projects firsthand, I often bring friends and colleagues along. I want to share the experience of meeting with elders, mothers and students, touring their farms and classrooms, hearing their stories and working alongside them to build something together. Whether we are laying the foundation of a new facility or placing the final bricks, the opportunity to connect with a cause is both grounding and inspiring. This experience has deeply touched my life and I believe everyone should have the chance to share in it.

ABOVE: *Peter Cordy (second from left) stands in front of the completed Mondaña Health Clinic with WE Charity staff Natalia Argoti (far left) and Ana Raquel Estrella (second from right), and clinic dentist Franciarge Mucura Monteverde (far right).*
FACING PAGE: *Minga Lodge overlooks the Napo River, the largest tributary leading into the Amazon River.*

In 2016, I traveled to the Ecuadorian Amazon with a group of employees from Klick Health, the business I co-founded more than two decades earlier. We stayed at WE Charity's Minga Lodge on the shores of the Río Napo, a tributary of the Amazon River. The WE organization partners with Indigenous communities in the region, historically marginalized groups that suffer from some of the highest rates of poverty in the country, and who lack access to clean water, education and economic opportunities. As a team, we were eager to work with WE Charity and community members

on an exciting new project—a health center in the middle of the rainforest.

The region previously had a floating hospital—a boat where nurses and doctors could treat patients in the riverside communities—but it was damaged and shut down. There was also a small clinic on land, but its simple wood construction was no match for the constant assault of rain and insects. The closest hospital was three hours away, an unmanageable distance for most, so families were forced to deal with illnesses on their own. Without treatment, even common ailments resulted in tragedy.

On our first morning in the rainforest, we were up at daybreak and ready to work, despite the 90-degree heat and humidity. We filled sandbags at the riverbank and hauled them uphill to the build site, where the old clinic had once stood. We must have made a hundred trips up and down that hill, and when we had moved enough sand, we sifted it and mixed the cement. Finally, with the help of local engineers and community members who had joined the crew, we started to build a wall. It was sometime in the middle of all that back-breaking work that a member of WE Charity's team made a surprising announcement. The health center we were building was actually being financed by one of my recent donations! That was a moment of true happiness for me. None of the material wealth in my life is as treasured as the feeling of being part of something that is making a difference in people's lives.

I returned to Ecuador in 2018 and visited the clinic. There I met a mother who had brought in her feverish toddler, and an elderly gentleman who had arrived with a toothache. In earlier days, they would have had nowhere to go for help. The new health clinic is equipped to offer maternal and family care and emergency and dental services; it is staffed by doctors, nurses and dentists—all supported by the Ministry of Health. Rather than a foreign intervention, it seemed to be completely at home in the rainforest, a part of community life that should have always been there.

This book is filled with stories of impact, and I had the great honor of contributing the photography. I traveled from Kenya to India to Ecuador alongside a writer and a translator. Communities welcomed us warmly, and I am grateful for every minute they shared with us. Though I still consider myself an amateur photographer, I sought to capture simple, honest moments, trying to walk in their footsteps, if not in their shoes. It has been an emotional experience for me to step into people's lives in such an intimate way. As I followed a teacher into her classroom or a farmer into his field, I realized again and again that if the lottery of our births had worked out differently, they might be holding the camera and I would be the one with bare feet.

I myself am not unfamiliar with struggle. As a young immigrant to Canada, I started out with very little and faced many challenges. But I was fortunate to find opportunities to succeed, so I feel it is my responsibility and obligation to create the same opportunities for others, no matter where they are in the world.

As a volunteer and supporter of WE Charity, I am proud to be working alongside Craig and Marc Kielburger, whose passion, vision and ingenuity have always inspired me. When I first read about them years ago, their story affected me deeply. Here were two kids who realized something was wrong in their world and were able to find a way to make a difference. I realized that if they could do it, it was also possible for me to do much more. So I have continued to channel my support through WE Charity, to enable projects that will have impact long into the future. And whatever I have shared has come back to me tenfold; resources and time have yielded a sense of fulfillment, joy and hope and an understanding that change is possible.

The Klick colleagues I have taken along with me on my travels have been some of the smartest, most productive leaders on our team. Taking them away from their work for any amount of time was an expensive investment, but I believe it was worth every cent. Every single person who has witnessed WE Charity's impact firsthand has told me that the experience opened their eyes, touched their hearts and even changed their outlook on life. And today each one is an ambassador for the development work that we are doing together.

My hope is that this book opens the same experience to readers, as not everyone is in the position to witness the impact in person. This book offers more than 30 stories of personal and community transformation—people picking up the tools to improve lives and creating incredible change. Behind each account are the thousands of supporters who have shared resources, time and energy to create opportunities for others to thrive. Without their support, we wouldn't have these stories to tell. But as more and more people of all means and ages find a way to connect with WE Charity's programs, and with the WE movement as a whole, I am hopeful that we will write a million more stories together.

Acknowledgments

"It takes a village to raise a child" is a well-known African proverb. This book is only possible because of the hard work, dedication and heartfelt commitment of the WE community—from our incredible teams in India, Kenya and Ecuador to our dedicated donors around the globe who are devoted to creating a more equitable world.

First off, to the individuals profiled within these pages, we thank you for letting us into your homes and opening your hearts. Thank you for trusting us with your stories, for sharing some of your most difficult days in order to show how your life has changed through your community's partnership with WE Charity. We are humbled to walk alongside you.

To our country teams in India, Kenya and Ecuador (whose work is showcased throughout this book) and our teams in Tanzania, Ethiopia, Nicaragua, Sierra Leone, rural China and Haiti: your vast knowledge, resourcefulness and relentless energy create impact every day. You form the relationships with our community partners that make this work possible, build trust through grassroots action and create vision through collaborations with local leaders and governments. WE Charity's ability to bring meaningful, sustainable change is only possible because of the contribution of every member of your teams, from drivers to mobilizers to program directors to engineers. *Dhanyawad. Asante sana. Gracias.*

A profound thank-you to Peter Cordy, who not only contributed the stunning photography in these pages but also originated the concept of this book and traveled through three continents to unearth stories of resilience and change. Your inspired vision and pursuit of excellence at every turn made this book a reality.

We are especially grateful to all the donors who have supported WE Charity's five-pillar sustainable development model: from the students and educators who've organized bake sales, lemonade stands and water walks, to the family foundations, individuals and corporations that have provided larger gifts to support major infrastructure. Your generosity has made all this possible. We celebrate you through these pages.

We owe a debt of gratitude to the architects of WE Charity's five-pillar development model. These visionaries recognized the need for a more integrated, holistic and thoughtful model to break the cycle of poverty and create an unstoppable momentum. That model has since increased access to education, clean water, health care, income opportunities and nutritious food for families around the world. A special thank-you to Lloyd Hanoman, Scott Baker, Robin Wiszowaty, Michael Wagner, Michelle Hambly, Erin Barton and Dalal Al-Waheidi.

Without the talented translators and fixers, the tales in this book would never have been told. These WE Charity team members know our projects intimately and journeyed with our writers to learn people's stories. In India, we are indebted to Ambrish Dubey, Manish Sharma, Raghavendra (Ricky) Ranawat and Hiranshi Bhatnagar; in Kenya, Zeddy Kosgei; and in Ecuador, Karloso Fiallos. Thank you for your grace, patience, good humor and insight.

Thank you to the fact-checkers, our gatekeepers of metrics-based impact reporting. We are so grateful to Iain Duncan and the WE Villages team in Toronto, who worked diligently with our writers to verify information and celebrate the transformative outcomes of communities in India, Kenya and Ecuador.

We are deeply grateful to Craig Burkinshaw, a steadfast champion of WE Charity's development model and our 25 years of work. He has enabled our global travel opportunities and been a passionate advocate for this book to share stories of impact. Thank you for your time, wisdom and efforts to broaden our community of supporters through the power of travel and cross-cultural connection.

We couldn't have accomplished any of this without our WE Charity Board of Directors, including Canadian Chair Michelle Douglas, US Chair Dr. Jonathan White and UK Chair Lord Rumi Verjee. Thank you for your endless support and guidance.

Thank you to our WE Day co-chairs, who pour passion and energy into empowering the next generation of change-makers. This incredible group includes our global WE Day Co-Chairs Dave I. McKay, David Aisenstat, Hartley Richardson and Craig Burkinshaw; National Co-Chairs in Canada Jennifer Tory, Darren Entwistle, Elio Luongo, Bill Thomas, Andrew Williams, Nelly Furtado, Jeffrey Latimer, the Honorable David C. Onley, Chief Perry Bellegarde, James Villeneuve and Mark Dervishian; National Co-Chairs in the US Steve Robinson and Janet Crown, Thomas J. Wilson and Jane Francisco; WE Day Alberta Co-Chairs Ed Sims, Bill and Sabrina Elkington, Rob Geremia and Leon Draisaitl; WE Day Atlantic Canada Co-Chairs Sean and Crystal Murray, Ken Power and Doug Reid; WE Day Baltimore Co-Chairs Ashton and Adair Newhall; WE Day California Co-Chairs Stephanie Argyros, Brett and Miranda Tollman, Patricia

Arvielo and Jeff Skoll; WE Day Illinois Co-Chairs Thomas J. Wilson, Alex Gourlay, Linda Imonti and Arne Duncan; and WE Day Manitoba Co-Chairs Hartley Richardson, Mark Chipman and Bob Silver.

We are grateful to the book team, who have combined the best in international development with the power of a good story. To editor-in-chief Shelley Page: your keen story sense strengthens every narrative you touch; your unwavering commitment to this book's potential started in its infancy and your meticulous eye never faltered. To writers Katie Hewitt, Wanda O'Brien and Deepa Shankaran: you each possess your own unique style and share a passion for telling stories that matter. You've done that here. To designer Linda Gustafson, your attention to detail and insightful eye make the pages come alive, breathe and let you settle in. To creative director Marta Cutler, thank you for your leadership, inspiration, direction and belief in the power of sharing WE's impact in this way. To project manager Sharon McAuley: your workback schedule and timelines kept us on track with poise and helpful nudges. Our long-time WE leader Kim Plewes propelled this book forward with her tenacious ability to connect individuals with causes to create a more just world. Thank you to copy editor Kate Lane-Smith for coming back to the WE family to work on this special project and guide these pages with your knowledge of the idiosyncrasies of language. To proofer Cheryl Hawley, thank you for your keen eye and agility. Also thanks to indexer and proofreader extraordinaire Gillian Watts.

To our parents, Theresa and Fred Kielburger, our earliest champions and strongest role models, who taught us about compassion and service—we are forever grateful. And for the unwavering support of our partners, Leysa Cerswell Kielburger and Roxanne Joyal, thank you is not enough. We love you more than words can ever express.

To all of you who have supported our five-pillar development model, none of this work would be possible without your partnership and your sustained belief in the power to do good. Thank you for joining us in this journey.

Index

Note: Page numbers in *italics* indicate photographs.

Join WE's journey of impact

If this book inspires you to be part of our story, whether that's to travel with us, to donate to our programs or even to volunteer your time, visit WE.org to learn how you can get involved. WE welcomes you.